What they're saying about

The Complete Guide to Bed & Breakfasts, Inns & Guesthouses...

...all necessary information about facilities, prices, pets, children, amenities, credit cards and the like. Like France's Michelin...
—New York Times

Definitive and worth the room in your reference library.
—Los Angeles Times

...innovative and useful...
—Washington Post

A must for the adventurous...who still like the Hobbity creature comforts.
—St. Louis Post-Dispatch

What has long been overdue: a list of the basic information of where, how much and what facilities are offered at the inns and guesthouses.
—San Francisco Examiner

Standing out from the crowd for its thoroughness and helpful cross-indexing...
—Chicago Sun Times

A quaint, charming and economical way to travel—all in one book.
—Waldenbooks (as seen in USA Today)

Little descriptions provide all the essentials: romance, historical landmarks, golf/fishing, gourmet food, or, just as important, low prices. Take your pick!
—National Motorist

For those travelling by car, lodging is always a main concern...The Complete Guide to Bed & Breakfasts, Inns & Guesthouses provides listings and descriptions of more than 1,200 inns.
—Minneapolis Star & Tribune

THE COMPLETE GUIDE TO

BED &
BREAKFASTS,
INNS & GUESTHOUSES

NORTHERN EDITION AND CANADA

PAMELA LANIER

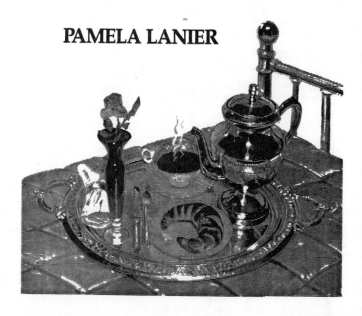

Other Books by Pamela Lanier

Alaska in 22 Days
All-Suite Hotel Guide
Elegant Small Hotels
Bed & Breakfast Cookbook

For further information, please contact:

The Complete Guide to Bed & Breakfasts,
  Inns and Guesthouses
P.O. Box 20467
Oakland, CA 94620-0467

John Muir Publications, P.O. Box 613, Santa Fe, NM 87504

© 1989 by John Muir Publications, Inc.
All rights reserved. Published 1989
Printed in the United States of America

1989-90 edition.

Cover by Jim Wood
Design & production by John Stick
Typography by Copygraphics, Santa Fe, NM

CONTENTS

VOTE

FOR YOUR CHOICE OF
INN OF THE YEAR

Did you find your stay at a Bed & Breakfast, Inn or Guesthouse listed in this Guide particularly enjoyable? Use the form in the back of the book or just drop us a note and we'll add your vote for the "Inn of the Year."

The winning entry will be featured in the next edition of **The Complete Guide to Bed & Breakfasts, Inns and Guesthouses in the U.S. and Canada.**

Please base your decision on:
- Helpfulness of Innkeeper
- Quality of Service
- Cleanliness
- Amenities
- Decor
- Food

Look for the winning Inn in the next Updated & Revised edition of **The Complete Guide to Bed & Breakfasts, Inns and Guesthouses in the U.S. and Canada.**

THE WEDGEWOOD INN
NEW HOPE, PENNSYLVANIA

When husband/wife team Carl Glassman and Dini Silnutzer first encountered the Wedgewood Inn, it was Bucks County's first Victorian painted lady, badly in need of refurbishment. Carl and Dini worked around the clock for two years restoring the inn room by room. Carl continued to commute to Princeton, New Jersey, for his job as a health researcher. Dini gave up her career as a social worker specializing in gerontology to devote herself to full-time innkeeping.

The Wedgewood Inn is painted in five shades of blue and white, with other Wedgewood colors, such as Jasper Pink, in the interior rooms, all of which contain an eclectic collection of antiques and Wedgewood china. The house itself was built in 1870 in high Victorian style on an older foundation dating from 1720 which once served as an encampment for George Washington's troops during the Revolutionary War.

Guests are greeted at the door by the inn's canine, Jasper, a three-year-old brown labrador, and treated to cookies and tea as they check in. Carl and Dini have produced their own map and mini-guide to the special attractions in New Hope which each guest receives.

Our readers love the special treatment they receive at the Wedgewood, starting with fantastic breakfasts, which may include freshly baked raspberry lemon muffins, hot cross buns, homemade jams and jellies, fresh fruit sundae with yogurt, or one of the hot croissants with herbs and cream cheese, all accompanied by freshly brewed tea and coffee. Breakfasts can be enjoyed luxuriously in bed or alfresco in one of the inn's gazebos. On Saturday and Sunday afternoon, guests gather by the fire in the parlor for a formal high tea and little goodies like finger sandwiches or maybe a white chocolate strawberry mousse.

Guests enjoy wandering through the stores at New Hope or socializing at the inn over croquet and board games. Nighttime brings a classic turn-down service with an almond liqueur and a chocolate mint.

Congratulations to Carl and Nadine, whose motto is "We treat everyone like royalty at the Wedgewood."

How to Use This Guide

How It's Organized

This book is organized alphabetically by state and, within a state, alphabetically by city or town. The inns appear first. At the back of the guide are a listing of the reservation service organizations serving each state and lists of inns with special characteristics.

Three Types of Accommodations

Inn: Webster's defines an inn as a "house built for the lodging and entertainment of travelers." All the inns in this book fulfill this description. Many also provide meals, at least breakfast, although a few do not. Most of these inns have under 30 guest rooms.

Bed and Breakfast: Can be anything from a home with three or more rooms to, more typically, a large house or mansion with eight or nine guest accommodations which serves breakfast in the morning.

Guest Houses: Private homes welcoming travelers, some of which may be contacted directly but mostly you reserve through a reservation service organization. A comprehensive list of RSO's appears toward the back of this guide.

Breakfasts

We define a **Full Breakfast** as one being along English lines, including eggs and/or meat as well as the usual breads, toast, juice and coffee.

Continental Breakfast means coffee, juice, bread or pastry.

Continental Plus is a breakfast of coffee, juice, and choice of several breads and pastry and possibly more.

Meals

Bear in mind that inns which do not serve meals are usually located near a variety of restaurants.

Can We Get A Drink?

Those inns without a license will generally chill your bottles and provide you with set-ups upon request.

Prices

We include a price code to give you an idea of each inn's rates. Generally, the coded prices indicate a given lodging's lowest priced double rooms, double occupancy rate as follows:

$—under $50 $$—$50-$75 $$$—$75 plus

Appearing to the right of the price code is a code indicating the type of food services available:

B&B: Breakfast included in quoted rate

EP (European Plan): No meals

MAP (Modified American Plan): Includes breakfast and dinner

AP (American Plan): Includes all three meals

All prices are subject to change. Please be sure to confirm rates and services when you make your reservations.

Credit Cards and Checks

If an establishement accepts credit cards, it will be listed as VISA, MC or AMEX. Most inns will accept your personal check with proper identification, but be sure to confirm when you book.

Reservations

Reservations are essential at most inns, particularly during busy seasons, and are appreciated at other times. Be sure to reserve, even if only a few hours in advance, to avoid disappointment. When you book, feel free to discuss your requirements and confirm prices, services and other details. We have found innkeepers to be delightfully helpful.

Arriving late: Most inns will hold your reservation until 6 p.m. If you plan to arrive later, please phone ahead to let them know.

Deposits or advance payment are required at some inns.

Children, Pets and Smoking

Children, pets and smoking present special difficulties for many inns. Whether they are allowed, limited, or not permitted, is generally noted as follows:

	Yes	Limited	No
Children	C-yes	C-ltd	C-no
Pets	P-yes	P-ltd	P-no
Smoking	S-yes	S-ltd	S-no
Handicapped	H-yes	H-ltd	H-no

Handicap Accessibility

Because many inns are housed in old buidlings, access for handicapped persons in many cases is limited. Where this information is available, we have noted it in the same line as limitations on children, pets and smoking. Be sure to confirm your exact requirements when you book.

Big City

In many big cities there are very few small, intimate accommodations. We have searched out as many as possible. We strongly advise you to investigate the guest house alternative, which can provide you with anything from a penthouse in New York to your own quiet quarters with a private entrance in the suburbs. See our RSO listings at the back of the book.

Farms

Many B&Bs are located in a rural environment, some on working farms. We have provided a partial list of farm vacation experiences. What a restorative for the city-weary. They can make a great family vacation— just be sure to keep a close eye on the kids around farm equipment.

Bathrooms

Though shared baths are the norm in Europe, this is sometimes a touchy subject in the U.S.A. We list the number of private baths available directly next to the number of rooms. Bear in mind that those inns with shared baths generally have more than one.

Manners

Please keep in mind when you go to an inn that innkeeping is a very hard job. It is amazing that innkeepers manage to maintain such a thoroughly cheeful and delightful presence despite the long hours. Do feel free to ask your innkeeper for help or suggestions, but please don't expect him to be your personal servant. You may have to carry your own bags.

When in accommodations with shared baths, be sure to straighten the bathroom as a courtesy to your fellow guests. If you come in late, please do so on tiptoe, mindful of the many other patrons visiting the inn for a little R 'n' R.

Price & included meals
Numbers of rooms and
   private baths
Credit cards accepted
Travel Agent commission ●
Limitations:
   Children (C), Pets (P)
   Smoking (S), Handicap Access (H)
Foreign language spoken

Name of Inn
Street address and Zip Code
Phone Number
Name of Innkeeper
Dates of operation

Name of city or town

Extra charge for breakfast

ANYPLACE —————————————————————————

Any Bed & Breakfast $$ B&B   Full breakfast ($)
Any Street, ZIP code   8 rooms, 6 pb   Lunch, dinner
555-555-5555   Visa, MC ●   sitting room
Tom & Jane Innkeeper   C-12+/S-ltd/P-no/H-ltd   library, bicycles
All year   French, Spanish   antiques

Large Victorian country house in historic village. Hiking, swimming and golf nearby. Old fashioned comfort with modern conveniences.

Description given by the innkeeper about the   Meals & drinks
original characteristics of his establishment   Amenities

Sample Bed & Breakfast Listing

Ejemplo de una entrada para las posadas con cama & desayuno

Ciudad o pueblo nombre

Nombre de la posada
Dirección
Teléfono
Fechas de temporada

Precio del alojamiento
Qué comidas van incluídas
Número de cuartos y número
   de cuartos con baño privado
Tarjetas de crédito aceptables
Limitaciones:
   niños (C); animales domésticos (P); prohibido
   fumar (S); entradas para minusválidos (H)
Se habla idiomas extranjeros

Comidas y bebidas
Entretenimientos

ANYPLACE ————————————————

Any Bed & Breakfast $$ B&B Full breakfast
Any Street, ZIP code 8 rooms, 6 pb Lunch, dinner
555-555-5555 Visa, MC • sitting room
Tom & Jane Innkeeper C-12 + /S-ltd/P-no/H-ltd library, bicycles
All year French, Spanish antiques

Large Victorian country house in historic village. Hiking, swimming and golf nearby. Old fashioned comfort with modern conveniences.

Descripción proporcionada por el dueño de la posada
sobre las características especiales y originales del
establecimiento

Mode d'emploi

Nom de ville

Prix des chambres Repas inclus ou non
Nombre de chambres et
chambres avec salle de
bain privés
Cartes de crédit acceptées

Repas, boissons possibles
Commodités

ANYPLACE ————————————————

Any Bed & Breakfast $$ B&B Full breakfast
Any Street, ZIP code 8 rooms, 6 pb Lunch, dinner
555-555-5555 Visa, MC • sitting room
Tom & Jane Innkeeper C-12 + /S-ltd/P-no/H-ltd library, bicycles
All year French, Spanish antiques

Large Victorian country house in historic village. Hiking, swimming and golf nearby. Old fashioned comfort with modern conveniences.

Nom de l'auberge
Addresse
Téléphone
Dates d'ouverture s'il n'y a
pas de dates ouvert toute
l'année

Restrictions
Enfants—Animaux
Fumeurs—Handicappés
On parle les langues etrangéres

L'aubergiste décrit ce qui rend son auberge unique

Erläuterung der Eintragungen der Unterkunfsstätte

Name der Stadt oder
Ortschaft

Name der Unterkunft
Adresse
Telefon-Nummer
Zu welcher Jahreszeit offen?

Preis für die Unterkunft, und
welche Mahlzeiten im Preis
einbegriffen sind
Anzahl der Zimmer, und
wieviel mit eigenem
Badezimmer (=pb)
Beschränkungen in Bezug auf
Kinder, Haustiere, Rauchen,
oder für Behinderte geeignet
(yes=ja; ltd=beschränkt;
no=nicht zugelassen)
Man sprecht fremdsprachen

Was für ein Frühstück?
Andere Mahlzeiten und Bars

Was gibt's sonst noch?

ANYPLACE

Any Bed & Breakfast
Any Street, ZIP code
555-555-5555
Tom & Jane Innkeeper
All year

$$ B&B
8 rooms, 6 pb
Visa, MC •
C-12+/S-ltd/P-no/H-ltd
French, Spanish

Full breakfast
Lunch, dinner
sitting room
library, bicycles
antiques

Large Victorian country house in historic village. Hiking, swimming and golf nearby. Old fashioned comfort with modern conveniences.

Beschreibung des Gastwirts,
was an diesem Gästehaus ein-
malig oder besonders
bemerkenswert ist

旅館名
住所
電話番号
利用期間。

都市又は町の名

朝食のタイプ
その他の設備
昼食、夕食、アルコールのサービス

ANYPLACE

Any Bed & Breakfast
Any Street, ZIP code
555-555-5555
Tom & Jane Innkeeper
All year

$$ B&B
8 rooms, 6 pb
Visa, MC •
C-12+/S-ltd/P-no/H-ltd
French, Spanish

Full breakfast
Lunch, dinner
sitting room
library, bicycles
antiques

Large Victorian country house in historic village. Hiking, swimming and golf nearby. Old fashioned comfort with modern conveniences.

Illinois

DECATUR

Hamilton House B&B Inn $ B&B   Full breakfast
500 W. Main St., 62522   5 rooms, 1 pb   Comp. tea, wine
217-429-1669   Visa, MC, AmEx •   Restaurant, Bar
Nancy C. Phillips   C-yes/S-yes/P-no/H-no   Sitting room
All year   German, Dutch   gift shop

Built in 1892, this Victorian mansion is on the National Register of Historic Places. Guest rooms filled with antique furniture.

EVANSTON

Charles & Barbara Pollard $ B&B   Continental breakfast
2633 Poplar, 60201   2 rooms, 1 pb
312-328-6162   C-yes/S-yes/P-ltd
Charles & Barbara Pollard
All year

Casual comfort and the location's a plus! Three blocks to Northwestern University's Dyche Stadium; walk to transportation, Lake Michigan, antiques, restaurants, movies and more!

The Homestead $$ EP   French restaurant
1625 Hinman Ave., 60201   35 rooms, 35 pb
312-475-3300   C-yes/S-yes/P-no/H-ltd
David T. Reynolds
All year

Historic residential neighborhood; two blocks from Lake Michigan & Northwestern Univ.; 30 minutes from Downtown Chicago by car or rail; French restaurant serves dinner.

GALENA

Aldrich Guest House $$ B&B   Full breakfast
900 Third Street, 61036   5 rooms, 3 pb   Comp. beverages
815-777-3323   Visa, MC   Sitting room w/fireplace
Judy Green   C-6+/S-ltd/P-no/H-no   piano, screened porch
All year

Elegant Greek Revival furnished with fine antiques. Breakfast in dining room or screened porch served formally yet unfussily. Central air-conditioning.

Avery Guest House B&B $ B&B   Continental plus
606 S. Prospect St., 61036   4 rooms   Afternoon tea or cider
815-777-3883   Visa, MC   Library
Flo & Roger Jensen   C-yes/S-no/P-no/H-no   sitting room
All year   porch swing

Enjoy historic Galena, scenic beauty, fine restaurants, antiques. Comfortable 1840's house, homey hospitality, porch swing, piano and sunny dining room.

Comfort Guest House
1000 Third St., 61036
815-777-3062
Connie & Tom Sola
All year

$$ B&B
3 rooms
C-14+ /S-ltd/P-no/H-no

Continental plus
Sitting room w/ fireplace
front porch

Riverfront town, home of Ulysses S. Grant. 1856 guest house. Stroll to downtown antique shops. Quilts, country breakfasts. Golf, skiing, biking nearby.

Mars Avenue Guest Home
515 Mars Ave., 61036
815-777-3880
Joanne Bielenda
February—December

$$ B&B
4 rooms
Visa, MC
C-12+ /H-yes

Continental plus
Afternoon tea
Sitting room

Relax in a country home in old Galena. Stenciling throughout. Near quaint shops, antiques and riverboat rides.

Stillman's Country Inn
P.O. Box 272, 61036
513 Boothillier
815-777-0557
Bill & Pamela Lozeau
All year

$$ B&B
5 rooms, 5 pb
Visa, MC
C-ltd/S-yes/P-no/H-no
German

Continental breakfast
2 Victorian dining rooms
2 cocktail lounges
nightclub
color cable TV

Stillman Manor Estate, 1858. General Grant was a regular guest. Antiques and fireplaces, crystal, porcelain. Riverboats.

Stillwaters Country Inn
7213 W. Buckhill Rd., 60613
815-777-0223
Honora Simon
All year

$$ B&B
3 rooms, 3 pb
●
C-yes/S-yes/P-no/H-no

Continental breakfast
Kitchens
Sitting room
sauna
special packages avail.

Unique guest suites in charming country hideaway—located on 17 secluded wooded acres only 5 miles from Galena, Illinois.

GENEVA

Oscar Swan Country Inn
1800 W. State St., 60134
312-232-0173
Nina Heymann
All year

$$$ B&B
8 rooms, 4 pb
Visa, MC ●
C-yes/S-no/P-no/H-no
German

Full breakfast
Snacks
Sitting room, library
tennis courts, pool
X-C skiing on 7 acres

Country hideaway on 7 private acres. Fireplaces, cozy kitchen, hearty breakfast, wonderful River Town, antiques, bike paths. The New England of the Midwest.

GOODFIELD

Brick House B&B
P.O. Box 301, 61742
RR 1, Conklin Court
309-965-2545/800-322-2304
Charles M. Conklin
All year

$ B&B/$$ MAP
4 rooms
S-yes

Full breakfast
Dinner-theatre (MAP)
Sitting room
riding stable nearby

Built in 1857; many of the original furnishings are still in the home where Abe Lincoln once spent his time. Dinner-theatre in old round roofed barn. In rural setting.

NAPERVILLE

Harrison House B&B	$ B&B	Full breakfast
26 N. Eagle St., 60540	4 rooms, 2 pb	Comp. wine, tea, snacks
312-420-1117 / 312-355-4665	Visa, MC, AmEx ●	Sitting room
Matthew & Elizabeth Preberg	S-ltd	bicycles
All year	Spanish	tennis & pool nearby

25 miles west of Chicago. Walk to quaint shops, restaurants. Antique guest rooms; Victorian Room has jacuzzi. Scrumptious breakfast and gracious hospitality.

ROCK ISLAND

Potter House B&B	$ B&B	Continental plus
1906-7 Ave., 61201	4 rooms, 3 pb	Afternoon tea
Nancy & Gary Pheiffer	Visa, MC	Library
All year	C-yes	tennis courts, pool
		& restaurant nearby

Historic landmark, circa 1907. Close to Mississippi River attractions. Breakfast served in mahogany paneled dining room or elegant sunporch.

Top O' The Morning	$ B&B	Full breakfast
1505 19th Ave., 61201	2 rooms, 2 pb	Sitting room, library
309-786-3513	C-yes/S-ltd/P-no/H-no	piano, bicycles
Sam & Peggy Doak		tennis, hot tubs
All year		A/C in all bedrooms

Brick mansion on 3½ acres in the center of town. Large porch, grand piano, formal dining. Irish hospitality. Champagne, flowers & breakfast in bridal suite for honeymoons.

More Inns. . .

Haagen House B&B 617 State St., Alton 62002 618-462-2419
Wright Farmhouse RR 3, Carthage 62321 217-357-2421
Davidson Place B&B 1110 Davidson Drive, Champaign 61820 217-356-5915
Colonia Inn Route 3, Dixon 61021 815-652-4422
River View Guest House 507 East Everett, Dixon 61021 815-288-5974
Hobson's Bluffdale Eldred-Hillview Rd, Eldred 62027 217-983-2854
Corner Nest B&B 3 Elm St., P.O. Box 22, Elsah 62028 618-374-1892
Green Tree Inn P.O. Box 96, 15 Mill St., Elsah 62028 618-374-2821
Belle Aire Mansion Rte. 20 West, Galena 61036 815-777-0893
Chestnut Mountain Resort 8700 W. Chestnut Rd., Galena 61036 800-435-2914
Colonial Guest House 1004 Park Ave., Galena 61036 815-777-0336
Hellman House 318 Hill St., Galena 61036 815-777-3638
Homestead 1022 Fourth St., Galena 61036 815-774-6963
Mars Ave Guest Home 515 Mars Ave., Galena 60067
Mother's Country Inn 349 Spring St., Galena 61036 815-777-3153
Robert Scribe Harris House 713 S. Bench St., Galena 61036 815-777-1611
Victorian Mansion 301 High St., Galena 61036 815-777-0675
Stolz Home RR 2, Box 27, Gibson City 60936 217-784-4502
Mansion of Golconda P.O. Box 339, Golconda 62938 618-683-4400
Colonial Inn Rock & Green Sts., Grand Detour 61021 815-652-4422
Carr Mansion Guest House 416 E. Broadway, Monmouth 61462 309-734-3654
Die Blane Gaus 95265 Route 59, Naperville 60565 312-355-0835
Inn-on-the-Square 3 Montgomery St., Oakland 61943 217-346-2289
Barber House Inn 410 W. Mason, Polo 61064 815-946-2607
Victoria's B&B 201 North Sixth St., Rockford 61107 815-963-3232
Mischler House 718 South 8th St., Springfield 62703 217-523-3714

Stage Coach Inn   41 W. 278 Whitney Rd., St. Charles 60174   312-584-1263
Maple Lane   3115 Rush Creek Rd., Stockton 61085   815-947-3773
Wheaton Inn   301 W. Roosevelt Rd., Wheaton 60187   312-690-2600
Bundling Board Inn   222 E. South St., Woodstock 60098

Indiana

BEVERLY SHORES

Dunes Shore Inn	$ B&B	Continental plus
Box 807, 46301	12 rooms	Comp. cider & cookies
Lakeshore County Rd.	Visa, MC	Library, sitting room
219-879-9029	C-yes/S-ltd/P-no/H-no	bicycles
Rosemary & Fred Braun	German	outdoor grill, tables
All year		

Located one block from Lake Michigan and surrounded by the National Lakeshore and Dunes State Parks, this inn is an oasis for nature lovers. One hour from Chicago.

COLUMBUS

Lafayette Street B&B	$ B&B	Full breakfast
723 Lafayette St., 47201	2 rooms, 1 pb	Afternoon tea by requ.
812-372-7245	C-yes/S-no/P-no/H-no	Snacks
Patti March & Mike Mullett		restaurant, tennis &
All year		library nearby

Charming, comfortable Queen Anne Victorian with period architectural features and antique furnishings. Over 40 outstanding examples of contemporary architecture nearby.

CORYDON

Kinter House Inn	$ B&B	Full breakfast
101 S. Capitol Ave., 47112	16 rooms, 16 pb	Snacks
812-738-2020	Visa, MC, AmEx, DC •	Tennis courts
Mary Jane Bridgewater	C-yes	golf arrangements
Exc. Thanksgiving, Xmas		swimming

National Historic Registry— 14 guest rooms in Victorian and country decor. Full breakfast. Located in downtown historic Corydon. 2 miles south of I-64.

CRAWFORDSVILLE

Davis House	$ B&B	Continental plus
1010 W. Wabash Ave., 47933	3 rooms, 3 pb	Snacks
317-364-0461	Visa, MC, AmEx •	Sitting room
Jan Stearns	C-yes/S-yes/P-no/H-no	library
All year		

Victorian mansion with country atmosphere near canoeing, hiking, and historical sites. Complimentary snacks. Homemade coffee cakes and breads for breakfast.

EVANSVILLE

Brigadoon B&B Inn	$ B&B	Full breakfast
1201 S.E. Second St., 47713	4 rooms, 2 pb	Stained glass
812-422-9635/812-425-1696	Visa, MC •	library, sitting room
Kathee Forbes	C-yes/S-yes/P-yes/H-yes	meeting rooms for
All year		parties, etc.

Romantic, lace-filled, river city Victorian. Picket fence, gingerbread porch, parquet floors, four fireplaces. Hearty breakfast, homemade breads.

FORT WAYNE

Candlewyck Inn
331 W. Washington Blvd., 46802
219-424-2643
Bob & Jan Goehringer
All year

$$ B&B
5 rooms
Visa, MC, AmEx •
C-no/S-ltd/P-no/H-no

Continental plus (wkdys)
Full breakfast (wkends)
Comp. wine & cheese
Sun porch, cable TV
bicycles

Charming, historical inn close to convention center and public library. Five lovely rooms, beautiful decor. Hearty continental breakfast.

GOSHEN

Checkerberry Inn
62644 County Road 37, 46526
219-642-4445
The Graff Family
Closed January

$$$ B&B
12 rooms, 12 pb
Visa, MC, AmEx •
C-yes/S-ltd/H-yes

Continental plus
Lunch/dinner, restaurant
Sitting room, library
tennis courts, pool
croquet court

European-style country inn surrounded by Amish farmland, 100 acres of fields and woods. French country cuisine, luxuriously comfortable decor.

HAGERSTOWN

Teetor House, Inn At Hagerstown
300 West Main St., 47346
317-489-4422
Jack & Joanne Warmoth
All year

$$ B&B
4 rooms, 4 pb
Visa, MC
C-yes/S-ltd

Full breakfast
Lunch & dinner (groups)
Afternoon tea, snacks
Sitting room, library
tennis courts, pool

Elegance and charm in a peacefully rural setting near unique shops and restaurants. Air conditioned. 5 miles from I-70. Golf courses nearby. Horse and buggy rides available.

INDIANAPOLIS

Barn House
10656 E. 63rd St., 46236
317-823-4898
Dr. Joe & Bettye Miller
All year

$ B&B
2 rooms, 1 pb
C-6+/S-yes/P-no/H-no

Continental plus
Kitchen

Charming, spacious guest house—living room, kitchen, bath, 2 bedrooms. Peace and quiet within half-hour of Indianapolis.

Hollingsworth House Inn
6054 Hollingsworth Rd., 46254
317-299-6700
Susan Muller & Ann Irvine
All year

$$$ B&B
5 rooms, 5 pb
AmEx, Visa, MC •
C-no/S-yes/P-no/H-no

Continental plus
Soft drinks
Sitting room

Country hideaway within the city; 1854 brick farmhouse furnished with antiques, beautiful linens and china. Listed on the National Register of Historic Places.

KNIGHTSTOWN

Old Hoosier House
Route 2, Box 299-1, 46148
Greensboro Pike & CR 750S
317-345-2969
Tom & Jean Lewis
May 1—November 1

$ B&B
4 rooms, 3 pb
•
C-yes/S-ltd/P-no/H-no

Full breakfast
Afternoon tea, snacks
Sitting room
library, bicycles
special golf rates

1840 country home near Indianapolis; popular antique area; comfortable homey atmosphere; delicious breakfasts on patio overlooking Royal Hylands Golf Club.

LA GRANGE

The 1886 Inn
P.O. Box 5, 46761
212 W. Factory St.
219-463-4227
The Billman Family
All year

$$ B&B
3 rooms, 3 pb
Visa, MC
C-yes/S-no/P-no/H-no

Continental plus
Sitting room
bicycles

Step back in time to the 19th-century style of living. Only 10 minutes from Shipshewana Auction and Flea Market in Indiana's Amish country.

METAMORA

Publick House
P.O. Box 219, 47030
28 Duck Creek Crossing
317-647-6235
Fred & Fern Betz
April 15—December 24

$ B&B
6 rooms, 4 pb
Visa, MC, DC •
C-yes/S-yes/P-ltd/H-yes

Continental breakfast

Circa 1850 frontier architecture, in a small country town. Enjoy the quiet atmosphere; walk to over 100 crafts and gift shops.

MIDDLEBURY

Bee Hive B&B
P.O. Box 1191, 46540
219-825-5023
Herb & Treva Swarm
All year

$ B&B
3 rooms
C-yes/S-no

Continental plus
Snacks
Sitting room
restaurant nearby

A country home in a relaxing atmosphere. Located in Amish Country with plenty of local attractions. Ski trails nearby. Easy access to Indiana Toll Road.

Old Hoosier House, Knightstown, IN

Patchwork Quilt Country Inn	$ B&B	Continental plus
11748 C.R. #2, 46540	6 rooms	Lunch, dinner
219-825-2417	C-12+/S-no/P-no/H-no	Sitting room
Maxine Zook		piano
All year		Amish tours

Prepare to be pampered in gracious country home; patchwork quilts on all beds. In Amish country. Near Shipshewana Flea Auction. Award winning Amish Backroad Tours.

MORGANTOWN

Rock House	$ B&B	Full breakfast
380 W. Washington St., 46160	6 rooms, 4 pb	Afternoon tea, snacks
812-597-5100	C-yes	Sitting room
Doug & Marcia Norton		
All year		

Circa 1894. Unusual Victorian home built of concrete block embedded with treasures: dishes, doorknobs, dice, marbles! Located at "The Gateway to Brown County."

NASHVILLE

Allison House Inn	$$$ B&B	Continental plus
P.O. Box 546, 47448	5 rooms, 5 pb	Library
90 S. Jefferson St.	C-6+/S-no/P-no/H-no	Sitting room
812-988-0814		
Bob & Tammy Galm		
All year		

In the heart of Brown County, the center for the arts and craft colony. Coziness, comfort and charm.

PLYMOUTH

Driftwood	$$$ B&B	Continental breakfast
P.O. Box 16, 46563	3 rooms, 3 pb	Sitting room
4604 Westshore Dr.	C-ltd/S-ltd/P-no/H-no	fireplace, TV in rooms
219-546-2274		swimming, canoeing,
May 1—October 31		biking & hiking nearby

Lakefront home decorated in casual nautical style with beautiful beach and summer recreation.

SHIPSHEWANA

Green Meadow Ranch	$ B&B	Continental plus
R 2, Box 592, 46565	7 rooms	Sitting room
219-768-4221	C-ltd/S-no/P-no/H-no	
Paul & Ruth Miller	Penn. Dutch	
Closed January & February		

Country home decorated with antiques, near famous flea market in Amish area. Miniature horses and donkeys, folk art.

SOUTH BEND

Queen Anne Inn	$$ B&B	Full breakfast
420 W. Washington, 46601	5 rooms, 5 pb	Snacks
219-234-5959	Visa, MC, AmEx ●	Sitting room
Pauline Medhurst	C-yes/S-ltd/P-no/H-no	library
All year		conference room (15-25)#

Relax in a charming 1893 Victorian home with Frank Lloyd Wright influence—near city center and many good restaurants.

WESTFIELD

Camel Lot
4512 W. 131st St., 46074
317-873-4370
Moselle Schaffer
All year

$$ B&B
1 room, 1 pb
C-10+/S-yes/P-no/H-yes

Full breakfast
Sitting room
piano

Have breakfast on the terrace overlooking the Siberian tiger's quarters—photograph zebras, llamas, deer at this exotic animal breeding ranch.

More Inns. . .

Open Hearth B&B   56782 SR 15, Bristol 46507   219-825-2417
Gray Goose Inn B&B   350 Indian Boundary Rd., Chesterton 46304   219-926-5781
Wingfield's Inn B&B   526 Indian Oak Mall, Chesterton 46304   702-348-0766
Sycamore Spring Farm   Box 224, Churubusco 46723   219-693-3603
Cragwood Inn   303 N. Second St., Decatur 46733   219-728-9388
The 1900 House   50777 Ridgemoor Way, Granger 46530   219-277-7783
De'Coy's B&B   1546 W. 100 N., Hartford City 47348   317-348-2164
Pairadux Inn   6363 N. Guilford Ave., Indianapolis 46220   317-259-8005
Ye Olde Scotts Inn   RR 1, Box 5, Leavenworth 47137   812-739-4747
Cliff House   122 Fairmount Drive, Madison 47250   812-265-5272
Millwood House   512 West St., Madison 47250   812-265-6780
The Thorpe House   Clayborne St., Metamora 47030   317-647-5425
Creekwood Inn   Rt. 20-35, Michigan City 46460   219-872-8357
Duneland Beach Inn   3311 Potawatomi, Michigan City 46360   219-874-7729
Coneygar   54835 C.R. 33, Middlebury 46540   219-825-5707
Beiger Mansion Inn   Mishawaka 46544
Indiana Amish Country B&B   1600 W. Market St., Nappanee 46550   219-773-4188
McGinley's Vacation Cabins   Rt. 3, Box 332, Nashville 47448   812-988-7337
Seasons   P.O. Box 187, Nashville 47448   812-988-2284
Story Inn   P.O. Box 64, Nashville 47448   812-988-6516
Sunset House   RR 3 Box 127, Nashville 47448   812-988-6118
Rosewood Mansion   54 N. Hood, Peru 46970   317-472-7151
Country Homestead Guest House   Rte. 1, Box 353, Richland 47634   812-359-4870
Jelley House Country Inn   222 S. Walnut St., Rising Sun 47404   812-438-2319
Victorian House   RR1 Box 27, Roachdale 46172   317-522-1225
Jamison Inn   1404 N. Ivy Rd., South Bend 46637   219-277-9682
Mayor Wilhelm's Villa   428 N. Fifth St., Vincennes 47591   812-882-9487
Hilltop House B&B   88 W. Sinclair St., Wabash 46992   219-563-7726
Amish Acres, Inc.   160 W. Market, Wappanee 46550   219-773-4188
Candlelight Inn   503 E. Fort Wayne St., Warsaw 46580   219-267-2906
Country Rd. Guesthouse   2731 W. 146th St., Westfield 46074   317-846-2376

Kentucky

BARDSTOWN

Talbot Tavern/McLean House $$ B&B
107 W. Stephen Foster Ave, 40004
502-348-3494
Bill & Jimmy Kelley
All year

11 rooms, 11 pb
Visa, MC, AmEx, DC
C-yes/S-yes/P-no/H-no

Continental breakfast
Lunch, dinner, bar
Entertainment
gift shop

1779 stone inn, one of first hostelries west, each room original, fireplaces, antiques. Wall paintings done by guest Prince Louis Phillipe of France.

BRANDENBURG

Doe Run Inn
Rte. 2, 40108
502-422-2982
Lucille S. Brown
All year

$-87
14 rooms, 5 pb
Visa, MC
C-yes/S-yes/P-no/H-no

Full breakfast
Lunch, dinner
Sitting room

Quiet country inn beside a running brook. Antiques. Breakfast, lunch & dinner daily, smorgasbords Friday night & Sunday noon. 1000 acres to wander in.

FRANKFORT

Olde Kentucke B&B Inn
210 E. Fourth St., 40601
502-227-7389
Patty Smith
All year

$ B&B
4 rooms, 3 pb
Visa, MC, AmEx ●
C-15+/S-yes/P-no/H-no

Continental plus
Afternoon tea
Sitting room, ceiling
fans, clawfoot tubs
third night free

Cheerful, old-fashioned boarding house atmosphere in historic district of Frankfort, which is nestled among the rolling hills of the Bluegrass region. 3rd night free policy.

GEORGETOWN

Log Cabin B&B
350 N. Broadway, 40324
502-863-3514
Janis & Clay McKnight
All year

$$ B&B
2 rooms, 1 pb
●
C-yes/S-yes/P-yes/H-yes

Continental plus
Complete kitchen
Entire cabin filled with
interesting amenities
fireplace, A/C

Authentic log cabin (1809); antique furnishings, complete kitchen, 2 bedrooms, fireplace, air conditioning; located 2 miles north of Lexington, 1.7 miles off I-75.

HARRODSBURG

Beaumont Inn
40330
606-734-3381
Chuck Dedman
March—November

$-87
29 rooms, 29 pb
Visa, MC
C-yes/S-yes/P-no/H-no

Full breakfast
Luncheon, dinner
Swimming pool
tennis courts
Sitting room, piano

Country Inn built in 1845 in the heart of Kentucky's Bluegrass Region, furnished with antiques, serving traditional Kentucky Southern cuisine.

LEXINGTON —————————————————————————

Rokeby Hall | $$$ B&B | Full breakfast
318 S. Mill St., 40508 | 4 rooms, 4 pb | Lunch & dinner on requ.
606-254-5770 | Visa, MC, AmEx | Comp. wine, tea, snacks
Amy Hackett | C-yes/S-yes | Cable TV, fireplaces
All year | | off-street parking

Elegantly restored 19th-century home in the historic South Hill District of downtown Lexington—a real taste of Bluegrass hospitality.

More Inns...

Bowling Green B&B   659 E. 14th Ave., Bowling Green 42101   502-781-3861
Broadwell B&B   Rt. 6, Box 58, Cynthiana 41031   606-234-4255
Ehrhardts B&B   285 Springwell Drive, Paducah 42001   502-554-0644

Michigan

ANN ARBOR —————————————————————————

Urban Retreat | $ B&B | Full breakfast
2759 Canterbury Rd., 48104 | 2 rooms | Comp. wine/snacks, bar
313-971-8110 | C-no/S-yes/P-no/H-no | Sitting room, library
Andre' Rosalik & Gloria Krys | | patio, picnic area
All year | | gardens, bicycles, A/C

Charming 1950's ranch home on quiet tree-lined street; furnished with antiques; adjacent to 127-acre meadowland park; minutes from major universities.

ANN ARBOR-SALINE —————————————————————

Homestead B&B | $$ B&B | Continental plus
9279 Macon Rd., 48176 | 6 rooms, 1 pb | Comp. wine & cheese
313-429-9625 | Visa, MC, Diners • | Library
Shirley Grossman | C-12+/S-yes/P-no/H-no | sitting room
All year | | A/C in some rooms

1851 brick farmhouse on 50-acre farm. Comfort, country and Victorian elegance. Superb breakfasts. Close to Ann Arbor, Ypsilanti, Greenfield Village, Detroit.

National House Inn, Marshall, MI

BROOKLYN

Chicago Street Inn
P.O. Box 546, 49230
219 Chicago St.
517-592-3888
Karen & Bill Kerr
All year

$$ B&B
4 rooms, 4 pb
Visa, MC
C-13+/S-ltd

Continental plus
Complimentary wine
Sitting room

1886 Queen Anne Victorian home, furnished with antiques. Located in quiet village in the foothills of the Irish hills. Antique shops and hiking trails nearby.

CEDAR

Hillside B&B
Rt. 1-A, W. Lakeshore Rd, 49621
Cedar
616-228-6106
Jan & Don Kerr
All year

$$ B&B
2 rooms
C-yes/S-yes/P-no/H-no

Continental plus
Sitting room
hiking trail
lake access nearby

Victorian farmhouse with original wood floors and oak trim. Located fifteen miles NW of Traverse City. Large rooms overlooking Lake Leelanau.

CHARLEVOIX

Bridge Street Inn
113 Michigan Ave., 49720
616-547-6606
Penny & Doug Shaw
All year

$$ B&B
9 rooms, 3 pb
●
C-no/S-no/P-no/H-no

Full breakfast
Close to beaches,
restaurants, shopping
boating

Recapture the grace and charm of a gentler era in this ca. 1895 colonial revival home. 3 stories decorated with unique and interesting antiques. Each room has different decor.

FENNVILLE ───────────────────────────

Hidden Pond Farm $$$ B&B   Full breakfast
5975-128th Ave., 49408   2 rooms, 2 pb   Guest use of home
616-561-2491   C-12+/S-yes/H-yes
Edward X. Kennedy
All year

B&B accommodations of quiet elegance. Two rooms with private baths, plus five common rooms, on 28 acres of private ravined grounds.

FLINT ───────────────────────────

Avon House B&B $ B&B   Continental plus
518 Avon St., 48503   3 rooms, 1 pb   Sitting room
313-232-6861   C-yes/S-yes/P-no/H-no   A/C
Arletta Minore   extended stay rates
All year

Enchanting Victorian home six blocks from Auto World & Water Street Pavilion. Music, fine dining, cultural center, performing arts close by.

HOLLAND ───────────────────────────

Old Wing Inn $ B&B   Continental plus
5298 E. 147th Ave., 49423   5 rooms, 2 pb   Sitting room
616-392-7362   Visa, MC
Chuck/Chris Lorenz   C-yes/S-ltd/P-no/H-no
May 1—November 1

Relax amidst rustic charm in Holland's oldest historic landmark home. Once an Ottawa Indian mission in 1839, this home was built in 1844-46. State & National Register.

Parsonage 1908 $$ B&B   Continental plus
6 E. 24th St., 49423   4 rooms   Sitting room
616-396-1316   •   TV, games
Bonnie Verwys   C-no/S-no/P-no/H-no   golf, tennis nearby
May—October

European-style B&B in town famous for May tulip festival. Marvelous alternative to motels for traveling businesswomen. Convenient to several major cities.

Witt House $$ B&B   Full breakfast
283 Fallen Leaf Lane, 49424   5 rooms, 2 pb   Afternoon tea
616-399-0877   •   Sitting room
David & Shirley Witt   C-yes   bicycles
All year   Dutch

Country home decorated with country antiques in gracious and historic Waikazoo Woods. Short walk from Lake Macatawa. Dutch breakfast.

KALAMAZOO ───────────────────────────

Hall House B&B $ B&B   Continental plus
106 Thompson St., 49007   5 rooms, 3 pb   Library
616-343-2500   Visa, MC, AmEx   sitting rooms
Pam & Terry O'Connor   C-12+/S-ltd/P-no/H-no   piano
All year

Exceptional overnight accommodations in a renovated Georgian Colonial Revival, near the city, on the edge of the Kalamazoo college campus.

Kalamazoo House
447 W. South St., 49007
616-343-5426
Annette & Louis Conti
All year

$$ B&B
11 rooms, 11 pb
Visa, MC, AmEx
C-ltd/S-no/P-no/H-yes

Continental breakfast
Complimentary wine
Sitting room
hot tubs

Relaxing hot tubs, fine Belgian antiques, beautiful architectural detail, a hotel of recaptured elegance. Walk to shops, restaurants, cultural events.

LAKESIDE

Pebble House
15093 Lakeshore Rd., 49116
616-469-1416
Jean & Ed Lawrence
All year

$$$ B&B
8 rooms, 6 pb
C-12+/S-yes/P-no/H-ltd

Scandinavian cont. plus
Library room, pergolas
screen house w/hammocks
fireplace, bicycles
tenn. cts, wooden walkwys

Ca. 1910 decorative block & beach pebble house. Arts & Crafts furniture & decorative items. Fireplace, woodstove, rocking chairs and a lake view. Like going home to Grandma's.

LANSING

Maplewood
15945 Wood, 48906
517-485-1426
Pat & Keith Bunce
All year

$ B&B
C-10+

Full breakfast
Comp. wine, tea, snacks
Sitting room, library
bicycles
swimming pool

Country house on 3-acre parcel; only minutes to state capitol and Michigan State University at East Lansing.

LEXINGTON

Governor's Inn
P O Box 471, 48450
7277 Simons St.
313-359-5770
Bob & Jane MacDonald
Memorial Day—Late September

$ B&B
3 rooms, 3 pb
C-12+/S-yes/P-no/H-no

Continental plus
Sitting room

Governor's Inn recreates the atmosphere of a turn-of-the-century summer home—wicker, iron beds, rockers on the shady porch.

LUDINGTON

B&B at Ludington
2458 S. Beaune Rd., 49431
616-843-9768
Grace & Robert Schneider
All year

$ B&B
4 rooms, 1 pb
Major credit cards •
C-yes/S-no/P-yes/H-yes
French, Spanish

Full country breakfast
Afternoon tea
Sitting room
piano
hot tub

Two miles from Lake Michigan, we have 125 acres for hiking, skiing, snowshoeing (showshoes provided). Creek and trout pond. Also room in remodeled barn loft.

White Rose Cntry Inn on Hamlin Lk
6036 Barnhart Rd., 49431
616-843-8193
Dave & Terry Rose, Sara & Lila
May 1—October 30

$$ B&B
7 rooms, 4 pb
Visa, MC
C-12+/S-no/P-no/H-no

Continental plus
Restaurant
Sitting room
lakeside
marina nearby

Hospitality and accommodations planned for country comfort. Outdoor activities include rafting, boating, canoeing, golfing, antiquing, fruit picking. Many guest services.

MANISTEE

Inn Wick-A-Te-Wah
3813 Lakeshore Dr., 49660
616-889-4396
Marge & Len Carlson
All year

$ B&B
4 rooms, 1 pb
•
C-ltd/S-ltd/P-no/H-no

Continental plus
Complimentary wine
Sitting room

Gorgeous view to Portage Lake and Lake Michigan Channel. All water sports, golf, and snow skiing nearby. Lovely, airy rooms with period furnishings.

MANISTIQUE

Marina Guest House
P.O. Box 344, 49854
230 Arbutus
906-341-5147
Margaret & Ruth Beach
May 1—November 1

$ B&B
6 rooms, 2 pb
•
C-ltd/S-no/P-no/H-no

Full breakfast
Snacks
Sitting room
library, bicycles
tennis courts

Established as B&B in 1922. Walk across to the local marina; one block from business district. View of lighthouse and Lake Michigan.

MARSHALL

National House Inn
102 S. Parkview, 49068
616-781-7374
Mike & Betty McCarthy
except Christmas Eve

$ B
16 rooms, 16 pb
Visa, MC, AmEx
C-yes/S-yes/P-no/H-no

Continental plus
Sitting room

Michigan's oldest inn lovingly restored with authentic antiques, located in Marshall, home of the Midwest's most striking examples of Victorian architecture.

PENTWATER

Pentwater Inn
Box 98, 49449
180 E. Lowell
616-869-5909
Janet R. Gunn
All year

$ B&B
6 rooms, 3 pb
C-yes/S-yes/P-no/H-no
German

Full breakfast
Complimentary wine
Sitting room
organ, Ping-Pong table
tandem bicycle

Quiet residential area, good for retreats & family reunions, close to town. Beautiful beach, charter boats, good fishing; skiing, snowmobiling, shopping.

PETOSKEY

Stafford's Bay View Inn
P O Box 3 G, 49770
613 Woodland Ave.
616-347-2771
Judy Honor
May—Nov./Xmas—March 30

$$$ B&B
20 rooms, 20 pb
Visa, MC, AmEx
C-yes/S-yes/P-no/H-yes

Full breakfast
Lunch, dinner, tea, wine
Sitting room
piano

Michigan Historic Site overlooking Little Traverse Bay. Victorian charm, exceptional cuisine, scenic drives, shopping, summer and winter recreation.

PORT SANILAC

Raymond House Inn
111 S. Ridge St., 48469
313-622-8800
Shirley Denison
May—October

$$ B&B
7 rooms, 7 pb
•
C-12+/S-ltd/P-no/H-no

Continental plus
Bicycles
Sitting room
pottery studio

112-year-old Victorian home furnished in antiques; on Lake Huron; marina, boating, salmon fishing, swimming; owner-artist's gallery. New studio of handmade pottery.

SAINT IGNACE

Colonial House Inn
90 N. State St., 49781
906-643-6900
Litaine Lewis, Marilyn Hurst
May—October 1

$ B&B
17 rooms, 12 pb
Visa, MC, AmEx
C-yes/S-yes

Continental plus
Sitting room
library

Charming Colonial Revival style home facing Mackinac Island, directly across from one of the ferries. Delightful breakfast served in parlor.

SAUGATUCK

Kemah Guest House
633 Pleasant, 49453
616-857-2919
Cindi & Terry Tatsch
All year

$$$ B&B
7 rooms
Visa, MC •
Spanish

Continental breakfast
Sitting room
library

Turn-of-the-century mansion sports a combination of Old World flavor, art deco and a splash of southwestern airiness.

Maplewood Hotel
P.O. Box 1059, 49453
428 Butler St.
616-857-2788
Donald Mitchell
All year

$ B&B
13 rooms, 13 pb
Visa, MC, AmEx
C-yes/S-yes/P-ltd/H-ltd

Continental plus
Restaurant, lunch by req
Hors d'oeuvres, bar
Sitting room, library
pool, jacuzzi, tennis

Gracious Greek revival hotel is a gleaming tribute to the 19th century. Inside, crystal chandeliers, antiques and period furniture make the hotel a perennial favorite.

Park House
888 Holland St., 49453
616-857-4535
Lynda & Joe Petty
All year

$ B&B
7 rooms, 7 pb
Visa, MC •
C-12+/S-yes/P-no/H-yes

Continental plus
Sitting room
TV, board games
3rd floor game loft

Country home with New England charm; built in 1857. National Historic Register Home. Near town, Lake Michigan beaches, paddleboat rides, dinner cruises, x-c skiing, golf.

Twin Gables Country Inn
P.O. Box 881, 49453
900 Lake St.
616-857-4346
Mike & Denise Simcik
All year

$ B&B
10 rooms, 10 pb
Visa, MC •
C-ltd/S-ltd/P-no/H-yes
Italian, French, Maltese

Continental plus
Refreshments
Fireplace, hot tub
whirlpool, bicycles, A/C
garden park, pond, pool

Country charm overlooking Kalamazoo Lake. 8 charming rooms, each in a delightful theme decor. Short walking distance to downtown. 3 cottages furnished in antiques also available.

Wickwood Inn
Box 1019, 49453
510 Butler
616-857-1097
Sue & Stub Lewis
All year

$$ B&B
11 rooms, 11 pb
Visa, MC, AmEx
C-no/S-yes/P-no/H-yes

Continental breakfast
Comp. beverages
Sunday brunch
Screened porch, patio
4 common rooms, bicycles

Truly elegant comfort in stately home on beautiful Lake Michigan yachting harbor. Laura Ashley decor, antiques, stunning common rooms. Featured in 9/86 Glamour Magazine.

Chicago Street Inn, Brooklyn, MI

TRAVERSE CITY

Linden Lea B&B	$$ B&B	Full breakfast
279 S. Long Lake Rd., 49684	2 rooms, 1 pb	Snacks
616-943-9182	•	Sitting room
Jim & Vicky McDonnell	C-yes	lake frontage, rowboat
All year	Spanish	sandy beach, raft

Wooded lakeside retreat with private sandy beach, rowboat & raft. Comfortable country furnishings, window seats, antiques & beveled glass throughout. Heavily wooded. Peaceful.

Warwickshire Inn	$$ B&B	Full breakfast
5037 Barney Rd., 49684	3 rooms, 3 pb	Comp. tea, wine
616-946-7176	•	Sitting room
Dan & Pat Warwick	C-8+/S-ltd/P-no/H-no	A/C in rooms
All year		

Antique-filled ca. 1900 country farm home overlooking Traverse City. Spacious, comfortable rooms. Warm congeniality in a rural setting.

UNION CITY

Victorian Villa Guesthouse	$$ B&B	Full breakfast
601 N. Broadway St., 49094	8 rooms, 6 pb	Full Victorian tea
517-741-7383	Visa, MC •	Sitting rooms
Ron & Sue Gibson	C-yes/S-no/P-no/H-no	piano, bicycles
All year		2 ac. landscaped grounds

Elegantly restored 1876 estate house with romantic accommodations. An opportunity to escape the 20th century. Special Victorian theme weekends

UNION PIER ─────────────────────────────────────

Inn at Union Pier $$$ B&B   Full breakfast
P.O. Box 222, 49129   15 rooms, 15 pb   Sitting room, library
9708 Berrien St.   Visa, MC   Swedish fireplaces
616-469-4700   C-yes/S-no/P-no/H-yes   baby grand piano,massage
Madeleine & Bill Reinke   bicycles, hot tub
All year

Elegantly furnished inn blends barefoot informality with all the comforts of a well-appointed country home. 200 steps from Lake Michigan.

───

More Inns...

Briaroaks Inn   2980 N. Adrian Hwy., Adrian   517-263-1659
Torch Lake B&B   10601 Coy St., Alden 49612   616-331-6424
Winchester Inn   524 Marshall St., Allegan 49010   616-673-3621
Olde Bricke House   P.O. Box 211, Allen 49227   517-869-2349
Old Lamplighter's Homestay   276 Capital Ave., N.E., Battle Creek 49017   616-963-2603
William Clements Inn   1712 Center (M-25), Bay City 48708   517-894-4600
Terrace Inn   216 Fairview Ave., Bay View 49770   616-347-2410
Brookside Inn   US 31, Beulah 49617   616-882-7271
Windermere Inn   747 Crystal Drive, Beulah 49617   616-882-7264
Big Bay Lighthouse B&B   No.3 Lighthouse Rd., Big Bay 49808   906-345-9957
PJ's B&B   722 North 29th St., Bilings 59101   406-259-3300
Silver Creek   4361 US-23, South, Black River 48721   517-471-2198
Celibeth House   Blaney Park, Rt 1,Box 58A, Blaney Park 49836   906-283-3409
H. D. Ellis Inn   415 W. Adrian, US 223, Blissfield 49228   517-486-3155
Calumet House B&B   P.O. Box 126, Calumet 49913   906-337-1936
Garden Gate B&B   315 Pearl St., Caro 48723   517-673-2696
Bay Bed & Breakfast   Rte. 1, Box 136A, Charlevoix 49720   616-599-2570
Belvedere House   306 Belvedere Ave., Charlevoix 49720   616-547-4501
Channel View Inn   217 Park, Charlevoix 49720   616-147-6180
Chandelier Guest House   1567 Morgan Rd., Clio 48420   313-687-6061
Oakbrook Inn   7256 E. Court St., Davison 48423   313-658-1546
Bannicks B&B   4608 Michigan Rd., Dimondale 48821   517-646-0224
Kirby House   294 W. Center St,Box 1174, Douglas 49406
Rosemont Inn   83 Lake Shore Dr., Douglas 49406   616-857-2637
Sunrise B&B   Box 52, Eastport 49627   616-599-2706
House on the Hill   P.O. Box 206, Lake St., Ellsworth 49729   616-588-6304
B&B at Lynch's Dream   22177 80th Ave., Evart 49631   616-734-5989
"Porches"   2297 70th St., Fennville 49408   616-543-4162
Pine Ridge   N-10345 Old US 23, Fenton 48430   313-629-8911
Botsford Inn   28000 Grand River Ave., Framington Hills 40824   313-474-4800
B&B at the Pines   327 Ardussi St., Frankenmuth 48734   517-652-9019
Hotel Frankfort   Main St., Frankfort 49635   616-882-7271
Trillium   611 South Shore Drive, Frankfort 49635   616-352-4976
Sylvan Inn   6680 Western Ave., Glen Arbor 49636   616-334-4333
White Gull Inn   P.O. Box 351, Glenn Arbor 49636   616-334-4486
Harbor House Inn   Harbor & Clinton Sts., Grand Haven 49417   616-846-0610
Highland Park Hotel B&B   1414 Lake Ave., Grand Haven 49417   616-842-6483
Lakeview Inn   P.O. Box 297, Grand Marais 49839   906-494-2612
Fountain Hill   222 Fountain, NE, Grand Rapids 49503   616-458-6621
Wellock Inn   404 S. Huron Ave., Harbor Beach 48441   517-479-3645
Harbour Inn   Beach Drive, Harbor Springs 49740   616-526-2107
Red Geranium Inn   508 E. Main St., Box 613, Harrisville 48740   517-724-6153

Widow's Watch B&B   401 Lake St., Box 271, Harrisville 48740   517-724-5465
Grist Guest House   310 E. Main St., Homer 49245   517-568-4063
Hansen's Guest House   102 W. Adams, Homer 49245   517-568-3001
Wellman Accommodations   205 Main St., Horton 49246   517-563-2231
Chaffin Farms B&B   3239 W. St. Charles Rd., Ithaca 48847   517-463-4081
Munro House B&B   202 Maumee St., Jonesville 49250   517-849-9292
Stuart Ave. B&B   405 Stuart Ave., Kalamazoo 49007   616-342-0230
Creative Holiday Lodge   1000 Calumet St., Lake Linden 49945   906-296-0113
Stagecoach Stop B&B   Box 18, 4819 Leonard Rd W, Lamont 49430   616-677-3940
Springbrook B&B   28143 Springbrook Dr., Lawton 49065   616-624-6359
Riverside Inn   302 River St., Leland 49654   616-256-9971
Ludington House   501 E. Ludington Ave., Luddington 49431   616-845-7769
Bogan Lane Inn   P.O. Box 482, Mackinac Island 49757   906-847-3439
E. E. Douville House   111 Pine St., Manistee 49660   616-723-8654
Margaret's B&B   230 Arbutus, P.O. Box 344, Manistique 49854   906-341-5147
Leelanau Country Inn   149 E. Harbor Highway, Maple City 49664   616-228-5060
McCarthy's Bear Creek Inn   15230 C Drive North, Marshall 49068   616-781-8383
Helmer House Inn   Rt. 3, County Rd. 417, McMillan 49853   906-586-3204
Mendon Country Inn   440 W. Main St., Mendon 49072   616-496-8132
Jay's Bed & Breakfast   4429 Bay City Rd., Midland 48640   517-631-0470
Morning Glory Inn   8709 Old Channel Trail, Montague 49437   616-894-8237
Country Chalet   723 S. Meridian Rd., Mount Pleasant 48858   517-772-9269
Woods & Hearth B&B   950 S. Third St., Niles 49120   616-683-0876
Yesterday's Inn   518 N. 4th, Niles 49120   616-683-6079
Plum Lane Inn   P.O. Box 74, Northport 49670   616-386-5774
Vintage House B&B   Box 424, 102 Shabwasung, Northport 49670   **616-386-7228**
Wood How Lodge   Rt. 1 Box 44E, Northport 49670   616-386-7194
Stonegate Inn   10831 Cleveland, Nunica 49448   616-837-9267
Haus Austrian   4626 Omena Point Rd., Omena 49674   616-386-7338
Mulberry House   1251 Shiawassee St., Owasso 48867   517-723-4890
Sylverlynd   3452 McBride Rd., Owosso 48667   517-723-1267
The Cozy Spot   1145 Kalamazoo, Petoskey 49770   616-347-3869
Gull's Way   118 Boulder Lane, Petoskey 49770   616-347-9891
Pebble Beach   496 Rosedale Ave., Petoskey 49770   616-347-1903
Terrace Inn   216 Fairview Ave., Petoskey 49770   616-347-2410
Bear & The Bay   421 Charlevoix Ave., Petoske 49770   616-347-6077
Lake St. Manor   8569 Lake St. (M-53), Port Austin 49467   517-738-7720
Victorian Inn   1229 Seventh St., Port Huron 48060   313-984-1437
Webber House   527 James St., Portland 48875   517-647-4671
Country Heritage B&B   64707 Mound Rd., Romeo 48065   313-752-2879
Tall Trees   Rt. 2, 323 Birch Rd., Roscommon 48653   517-821-5592
Montague Inn   1581 S. Washington Ave., Saginaw 48601   517-752-3939
Jann's Guest House   132 Mason St., Box 301, Saugatuck 49453   616-857-8851
Kirby House   Box 1174, 294 W.Center St, Saugatuck 49453   616-857-2904
Newnham Inn   Box 1106, 131 Giffith St., Saugatuck 49453   616-857-4249
Rummel's Tree Haven   41 N. Beck St., Sebewaing 48759   517-883-2450
Old Harbor Inn   515 Williams St., Sough Haven 49090   616-637-8480
A Country Place B&B   Rt. 5,Box 43,N. Shore Dr., South Haven 49090   616-637-5523
Last Resort B&B Inn   86 North Shore Dr, South Haven 49090   616-637-8943
Ross B&B House   229 Michigan AVe, South Haven 49090   616-637-2256
Victoria Resort   241 Oak, South Haven 49090   616-637-6414
Alberties Waterfront   18470 Main St-North Shore, Spring Lake 49456   616-846-4016
Seascape B&B   20009 Breton, Spring Lake 49456   616-842-8409
Shifting Sands   19343 North Shore Drive, Spring Lake 49456   616-842-3594
Murphy Inn   505 Clinton Ave., St. Clair 48079   313-329-7118
Pink Palace Farms   6095 Baldwin Rd., Swartz Creek 48473   313-655-4076

Blvd. Inn   904 W. Chicago Blvd., Tecumseh 49286   517-423-5169
Cider House B&B   5515 Barney Rd., Traverse City 49684   616-947-2833
L'DA RU B&B   4370 N. Spider Lake Rd., Traverse City 49684   616-946-8999
Neahtawanta Inn   1308 Neahtawanta Rd., Traverse City 49684   616-223-7315
Queen Anne's Castle   500 Webster, Traverse City 49684   616-946-1459
Bear Haven   2947 4th St., Trenton 48183   313-675-4844
Gordon Beach Inn   16240 Lakeshore Rd., Union Pier 49129   616-469-3344
Green Inn   4045 West M-76, West Branch 48661   517-345-0334
River Haven   9222 St. Joe River Rd., White Pigeon 49099   616-483-9104

Minnesota

CANNON FALLS

Quill & Quilt, B&B	$$ B&B/MAP	Full breakfast
615 W. Hoffman St., 55009	4 rooms, 4 pb	Dinner by arrangement
507-263-5507	Visa, MC •	Comp. wine, sitting room
Denise Anderson, David Karpinski	C-12+/S-ltd	library, cable TV, games
All year		bikes, rec. room, deck

1897 Colonial revival home. Four guestrooms, suite with whirlpool. In scenic Cannon River Valley; near biking, hiking, skiing, canoeing, etc. 1 hour from Minneapolis/St. Paul.

EXCELSIOR

Christopher Inn	$$ B&B	Full breakfast
201 Mill St., 55331	8 rooms, 6 pb	Catered meals
612-474-6816	•	Sitting room
Howard & Joan Johnson	C-ltd/S-no/P-ltd/H-yes	grass tennis court
All year		bicycles

1887 Victorian mansion across from Lake Minnetonka, furnished with antiques and Laura Ashley prints. Guest rooms have sitting areas, 3 have fireplaces.

GRAND MARAIS

Pincushion Mountain B&B	$$ B&B	Full breakfast
P.O. Box 181, 55604	4 rooms, 1 pb	Lunch, Aft. tea, snacks
Gunflint Trail	Visa, MC •	Sitting room, library
218-387-1276/800-542-1226	C-13+/S-no/P-no/H-no	hiking, fishing
Scott & Mary Beattie		x-c skiing
Exc. April		

B&B sits on ridge of Sawtooth Mountains overlooking north shore of Lake Superior 1,000 feet below. Hiking & X-C ski trails at doorstep. 20 min. from Boundary Water Canoe Area.

HASTINGS

Thorwood Inn	$ B&B	Full breakfast
4th & Pine, 55033	8 rooms, 8 pb	Comp. evening snack
612-437-3297	Visa, MC, AmEx •	Sitting room, library
Dick & Pam Thorsen	C-yes/S-ltd/P-no/H-no	victrolas, fireplaces
All year		whirlpools

1880 French Second Empire home, listed on National Register. Suite-size rooms, feather comforters, fine local wine with evening snack.

LAKE CITY

Red Gables Inn
403 N. High St., 55041
612-345-2605
Bill & Bonnie Saunders
All year

$ B&B
4 rooms, 2 pb
Visa, MC •
C-13+/S-ltd/P-no/H-no

Victorian brkfast buffet
Comp. wine, snacks
Sitting room, library
bicycles
tennis nearby

Graciously restored 1865 Victorian on the shores of the Mississippi River. Enjoy antique decor, quiet elegance and Victorian breakfast. Sailing, swimming, skiing.

LANESBORO

Mrs. B's Historic
Lanesboro Inn
P.O. Box 411, 55949
101 Parkway
507-467-2154
Nancy, Jack, Grant & Kirk Bratrud

All year
9 rooms, 9 pb
S-ltd
some Norwegian, Hebrew

Full breakfast
Lunch & dinner by resv.
Comp. wine, snacks
Sitting room, library
tennis & golf nearby

Nestled deep in Root River Valley; 1872 limestone building in village on National Register. Serene; rural; famous for regional cuisine.

MINNEAPOLIS

Evelo's B&B
2301 Bryant Ave. S, 55405
612-374-9656
David & Sheryl Evelo
All year

$ B&B
3 rooms
C-yes/S-no/P-no/H-no

Full breakfast
TV, refrigerator
Coffee maker

1897 Victorian, period furnishings. Located on bus line, walk to Guthrie Theater, Minneapolis Art Institute, children's theater. Near historic Lake District.

NEW PRAGUE

Schumacher's New Prague
Hotel
212 W. Main St., 56071
612-758-2133/612-445-7285
John & Kathleen Schumacher
All year

$$$ EP
11 rooms, 11 pb
Visa, MC, AmEx •
C-no/S-yes/P-no/H-ltd

Full breakfast $
Lunch, dinner, bar
Sitting room, piano
front porch, gift shop
whirlpools, fireplaces

11 European decorated sleeping rooms named after the months of the year. Restaurant serves Czechoslovakian and German cuisine seven days a week.

NORTHFIELD

Archer House
212 Division St., 55057
507-645-5661/800-247-2235
Mary Lethbridge, Dallas Haas
All year

$ EP
28 rooms, 28 pb
Visa, MC, AmEx •
C-yes/S-yes/P-no/H-no

Continental plus $
Full service restaurant
sitting room, whirlpools
ski, bike, hike trails &
whirlpl suites, near golf

Historic 1877 inn, turn-of-the-century handcarved pine furniture, thick quilts, veranda. Northfield—the town that defeated Jesse James.

ORR

Kettle Falls Hotel, Inc.
Box 1272, Intern'tl Falls, 55771
Ash River Trail
218-374-3511
Charles & Rebecca Williams
May 15—October 1

$$$ EP/MAP
12 rooms
Visa, MC
C-yes/S-yes

Restaurant, bar service
Lunch, dinner, snacks
Sitting room
boating, hiking
canoeing

Listen to the loon's call at scenic, peaceful, historic Kettle Falls, snuggled in the wilderness of Voyageurs National Park.

RAY

Bunt's B&B	$$ B&B	Continental breakfast
Lake Kabetogama, 56669	3 rooms, 2 pb	Custom billiard table
218-875-3904	Visa, MC	stone fireplace, decks
Robert F. Buntrock	C-yes/S-yes/H-yes	gas BBQ, hot tubs, sauna
All year		motor boat, snowmobiles

Luxury accommodations near Voyageurs National Park near Canadian border. Hidden on 20 wooded acres; miles of marked hiking, snowmobile & X-C ski trails. Sportsman's paradise.

ROCHESTER

Canterbury Inn B&B	$$ B&B	Full breakfast
723 2nd St. SW, 55902	4 rooms, 4 pb	Comp. tea, wine
507-289-5553	Visa, MC, AmEx ●	Hors d'vs., sitting room
Jeffrey Van Sant	C-ltd/S-ltd/P-no/H-no	tv, stereo, cassettes
All year	Italian	

Victorian charm, modern comforts. Fireplace, a/c, phones. Gourmet breakfasts any time. Elegant "tea." Perfect for vacation, business visitors, Mayo Clinic.

SAINT PAUL

Chatsworth B&B	$$ B&B	Continental plus
984 Ashland Ave., 55104	5 rooms, 2 pb	Sitting room
612-227-4288	C-yes	library
Donna & Earl Gustafson		2 rooms with whirlpools
All year		

Peaceful retreat in city near Governor's Mansion. Whirlpool baths, down comforters, lace curtains. Excellent restaurants and unique shops within walking distance.

SAUK CENTRE

Palmer House Hotel	$ EP	Full service restaurant
500 Sinclair Lewis Ave., 56378	37 rooms, 4 pb	Tennis courts
612-352-3431	C-yes/S-yes/P-yes/H-no	sitting room, piano
Al Tingley	German	dinner theatre
All year		

Historic site—the "original Main Street" home of Sinclair Lewis—first American author to win the Nobel Prize for Literature.

SPRING VALLEY

Chase's	$$ B&B	Full farm breakfast
508 N. Huron Ave., 55975	5 rooms, 2 pb	Complimentary tea
507-346-2850	Visa, MC ●	Library
Bob & Jeannine Chase	C-yes/S-no/P-no/H-no	sitting room
May 1—November 1		crochet

Antiques throughout Chase's 19th-century mansion. Sleep in solitude, breakfast in quietness. Scenic southeastern Minnesota bluff country.

STILLWATER

Overlook Inn B&B	$$ B&B	Continental plus
210 E. Laurel, 55082	4 rooms, 2 pb	Complimentary wine
612-439-3409	H-yes	Sitting room, library
David & Janel Belz		small wedding receptions
All year		large screened porch

An 1859 Victorian home overlooking the St. Croix River Valley. Each guest room has its own unique river view.

Rivertown Inn	$ B&B	Cont. plus, Buffet wknds
306 W. Olive St., 55082	9 rooms, 6 pb	Social hour in evenings
612-430-2955	Visa, MC •	Sitting areas, bicycles
Chuck & Judy Dougherty	C-12+/S-ltd/P-no/H-no	screen porch, gazebo
All year		ski packages

The perfect getaway for all seasons, within walking distance of historic Stillwater and the pic-turesque St. Croix River, 30 minutes from Minneapolis.

WALKER ─────────────────────────────

Chase On The Lake Lodge	$ B&B	Full breakfast
P.O. Box 206, 56484	20 rooms, 20 pb	Lunch, dinner
6th & Cleveland	Visa, MC, AmEx, DC •	Restaurant, bar
218-547-1531	C-yes/S-yes/P-no/H-yes	Tennis nearby
James & Barb Aletto	Spanish, French	beach
All year		

Historic inn featuring fine dining with a spectacular view! Nightly entertainment in season.

More Inns...

Thayer Hotel   Hwy. 55, Annandale 55302   612-274-3371
Rainy River Lodge   Baudette 56623   218-634-2730
Basswood Hill's Farm   Rte. 1, Box 331, Cannon Falls 55009   507-778-3259
Mansion   3600 London Rd., Duluth 55804   218-724-0739
Murray St. Gardens B&B   22520 Murray St., Excelsior 55331   612-474-8089
East Bay Hotel   Box 246, Grand Marais 55604   218-387-2800
Gunflint Lodge   Box 100 GT, Grand Marais 55604   800-328-3325
Naniboujou Lodge   Star Rte. 1, Box 505, Grand Marais 55604   218-387-2688
Young's Island   Gunflint Tr. 67-1, Grand Marais 55604   218-388-4487
Rahilly House   304 S. Oak St., Lake City 55041   612-345-4664
Cosgrove   228 S. Second St., Le Sueur 56058   612-665-2763
Pine Edge Inn   308 First St. SE, Little Falls 56345   612-632-6681
Grand Old Mansion   501 Clay St., Mantorville 55955   507-635-3231
American House   410 E. Third St., Morris 56267   612-589-4054
Schuyten Guest House   257 Third Ave., Newport 55055   612-459-5698
Lowell House   RR 2 Box 177, 531 Wood, Old Frontenac 55026   612-345-2111
Pratt Taber Inn   706 W. 4th, Red Wing 55066   612-388-5945
St. James Hotel   406 Main St., Red Wing 55066   612-388-2846
Grant House   Box 87, Rush City 55069   612-358-4717
Country B&B   32030 Ranch Tr., Shafer 55074   612-257-4773
Kings Oakdale Park G.H.   6933 232nd Ave NE, Stacy 55029   612-462-5598
Driscolls for Guests   1103 South 3rd St., Stillwater 55082   612-439-7486
Hudspeth House B&B   21225 Victory Lane, Taylors Falls 55084   612-465-5811
Old Taylors Falls Jail   102 Government Rd., Taylors Falls 55084   612-465-3112
Hotel and Zach's   3rd & Johnson, Winona 55987   507-452-5460

Ohio

AKRON

Portage House
601 Copley Rd., 44320
216-535-1952
Harry & Jeanne Pinnick
February 1—November 30

$ B&B
5 rooms, 1 pb
C-yes/S-ltd/P-ltd/H-no
French, Spanish

Full breakfast
Sitting room, piano

Old Tudor-style house in historic setting of Indian portage between 2 river systems and the site of Akron's founding family. Homemade breads & jam.

CENTERVILLE

Yesterday B&B
39 S. Main St., 45458
513-433-0785
Barbara Monnig
closed varied vacations

$$ B&B
3 rooms, 3 pb
Visa, MC
C-12+ /S-ltd

Continental plus
Beverage on arrival
Fruit bowl in parlor
Sitting room
one suite

Beautifully restored Victorian home in historic district. Short drive to downtown Dayton, Air Force Museum, King's Island Amusement Park, antique centers.

DANVILLE

White Oak Inn
29683 Walhonding Rd., 43014
614-599-6107
Joyce & Jim Acton
All year

$$ B&B
7 rooms, 7 pb
Visa, MC
C-no/S-no/P-no/H-no

Full breakfast
Comp. sherry
Afternoon snacks
Dinner with notice
Sitting room

Large country home nestled in the hills of the Walhonding Valley. The Kokosing River provides fishing, canoeing and peaceful respites. Comfortable antique decor.

DELLROY

Pleasant Journey Inn
4247 Roswell Rd. SW, 44620
216-735-2987
Jim & Marie Etterman
All year

$ B&B
4 rooms, 1 pb
Visa, MC
C-10+

Continental plus
Sitting room

Restored Civil War mansion, furnished with antiques. Country charm close to swimming, boating, tennis and golf. Owners are retired Navy couple.

HURON

Captain Montague's Guests
229 Center St., 44839
419-433-4756
April—October

$$ B&B
6 rooms, 6 pb
C-13+

Continental plus
Lunch (picnic basket)
Afternoon tea, snacks
Swimming pool
garden & gazebo

Captain Montague's Guest House is near a summer theatre, waterfront parks, a boat harbor and Cedar Point. Ideal for reunions, weekend relaxing, or vacation travel.

KINSMAN

Hidden Hollow B&B
9340 State Rt. 5 N.E., 44428
216-876-8686
Rita White
All year

$ B&B
4 rooms, 3 pb
C-yes/S-yes/P-ask/H-no

Full breakfast
Complimentary wine
Sitting room
swimming pool

Lovely setting. Breakfast by the pool or on the balcony overlooking Hidden Hollow. Gourmet snacks.

MEDINA

Oakwood B&B
226 N. Broadway, 44256
216-723-1162
Lonore/David Charbonneau
All year

$ B&B
2 rooms
C-12+/S-ltd/P-no/H-no

Continental plus
Complimentary wine
Parlor
bicycles

Cozy country Victorian furnished with antiques, walking tour of restored Victorian village, antique shopper's paradise.

MiLLERSBURG

Inn at Honey Run
6920 County Rd 203, 44654
216-674-0011/800-468-6639
Marjorie H. Stock
exc. January 2-15

$$ B&B
36 rooms, 36 pb
Visa, MC, AmEx
S-ltd/H-ltd
German

Continental plus
Lunch/dinner (Mon-Sat)
Rest., sitting room
horseshoes
badminton, volley ball

A unique contemporary inn. 12 deluxe "cave" rooms feature spectacular views. Bird-watcher's delight. Located in Ohio's Amish country. Enjoy our traditional "country" cuisine.

MOUNT VERNON

Russell-Cooper House
115 E. Gambier St., 43050
614-397-8638
Tim & Maureen Tyler
All year

$$ B&B
6 rooms, 6 pb
C-13+/S-ltd/P-no/H-no

Full breakfast
Comp. wine, tea
Tea room for party/mtgs.
Porch, museum & shop
recreational assistance

Victorian elegance abounds in restored Gothic mansion! Antiques, memorabilia, museum/shop, delightful breakfasts in Ohio's colonial city. Special weekenders with dinner.

OLD WASHINGTON

Zane Trace B&B
Box 115, 43768
Main St.
614-489-5970/301-757-4262
Ruth D. Wade
May 1—October 31

$ B&B
4 rooms
C-yes/S-yes/P-no/H-ltd

Continental breakfast
Sitting room
heated swimming pool

On historic national trail, this 1859 Victorian brick home has charm aplenty. Near Zane Grey Museum.

POLAND

Inn At The Green	$ B&B	Continental breakfast
500 S. Main St., 44514	4 rooms, 2 pb	Complimentary wine
216-757-4688	Visa, MC •	Sitting room, deck
Ginny & Steve Meloy	C-11+/S-no/P-no/H-no	library, patio
All year		garden room

Authentically restored Victorian townhouse in preserved Western Reserve village near Youngstown. Convenient to Turnpike and I-80. Antiques, fireplace, oriental rugs, garden.

SANDUSKY

Bogart's Corner B&B	$ B&B	Full breakfast
1403 E. Bogart Rd., 44870	5 rooms	Comp. coffee, tea
419-627-2707	•	2 sitting rooms
Zendon & Davilee Willis	C-yes/S-yes/P-ask/H-no	large living room
May 1—October 1		10 min. to Cedar Point

Country charm near main roads; accessible to vacation activities or relaxation. Country breakfast in large kitchen. Enjoy Lake Erie and what it offers.

Pipe Creek B&B	$ B&B	Full breakfast
2719 Columbus Ave., 44870	3 rooms, 2 pb	Complimentary wine
419-626-2067	C-12+/S-yes/P-no/H-no	Sitting room
Beryl Dureck	some German	large library
Open May—October		

Century-old Queen Anne Victorian, furnished in antiques, large comfortable rooms. Lake Erie islands, Cedar Point Amusement Park close by. Many trees, birds & wildlife.

SPRING VALLEY

3 B's B&B	$ B&B	Full breakfast
103 Race St., 45370	5 rooms	Supper, tea, wine
513-862-4278/513-862-4241	C-yes/S-yes/P-yes/H-ltd	Sitting room
Patricia & Herb Boettcher		bicycles
All year		air-conditioned

Relax in this charming village home—owners retired Air Force couple. Twenty miles from Dayton's Air Force Museum, King's Island. Choice of Victorian or restored farmhouse.

TROY

H.W. Allen Villa B&B	$$ B&B	Full breakfast
434 S. Market St., 45373	5 rooms, 4 pb	Comp. wine, aftn. tea
513-335-1181	Visa, MC •	Self-serve snacks
Robert W. Smith	C-yes	Music room, bicycles
All year		front porch (smoking)

1874 restored Victorian mansion with antiques throughout; television; central A/C; 3 wineries; historic town; 20 minutes from Dayton; I-70 and I-75 access.

WAVERLY

Governor's Lodge	$ B&B	Continental plus
SR 552, 45690	9 rooms, 9 pb	Restaurant next door
Lake White	MC	Meeting space
614-947-2266	C-yes/S-yes/P-no/H-yes	bicycles, lake fishing
Dave James		lake boating & swimming
All year		

Country home style with private rooms. Great for getaways and reunions. On quiet peninsula. Close to recreation. Lake view from all rooms.

WEST MILTON

Locust Lane Farm B&B	$ B&B	Full breakfast
5590 Kessler	2 rooms, 1 pb	Afternoon tea
Cowlesville, 45383	C-yes/S-no/P-no/H-no	Library, sitting room
513-698-4743		screened porch
Ruth Shoup		bicycles
All year		

Comfort and hospitality in a tastefully decorated old home. Country farm setting. Gourmet breakfast served in dining room or screened porch.

ZOAR

Cobbler Shop Inn	$$ B&B	Full breakfast
#22, P.O. Box 511, 44697	5 rooms, 1 pb	Snacks
2nd & Main Sts.	Visa, MC, AmEx ●	Sitting room
216-874-2600	C-6+ /S-ltd/P-no/H-no	
Marian Worley		
All year		

Original structure in historic village, furnished in 18th- and 19th-century antiques; close to local museum and a number of charming shops.

Cowger House #9	$$ B&B	Full country breakfast
#9 4th St., 44697	3 rooms, 3 pb	Lunch & dinner by resv.
216-874-3542	●	Entertainment
Mary & Ed Cowger	C-yes/S-yes/P-no/H-no	honeymoon suite with
All year		fireplace & jacuzzi

A little bit of Williamsburg. 1817 log cabin with 2-acre flower garden maintained by the Ohio Historic Society.

More Inns. . .

Frederick Fitting House   72 Fitting Ave., Bellville 44813   419-886-4283
Rockledge Manor   Rt.3, Possum Run Rd., Bellville 44813   419-892-3329
McNutt Farm II/Outdoorsman Ldg.   6120 Cutler Lake Rd., Blue Rock 43720   614-674-4555
Chillicothe B&B   202 S. Paint St., Chillicothe 45601   614-772-6848
Slavka's B&B   180 Reinhard Ave., Columbus 43206   614-443-6076
Hill View Acres B&B   7320 Old Town Rd., East Fultonham 43735   614-849-2728
Granville Inn   314 E. Broadway, Granville 43023   614-587-3333
Beatty House   South Shore Dr., Kelley's Island 43438   419-746-2379
Cricket Lodging   Lakeshore Dr., Kelley's Island 43438   419-746-2263
Quiet Country B&B   14758 TWP Rd 453, Lakeville 44638   216-378-3882
White Fence Inn   8842 Denmanu Rd., Lexington 44904   419-884-2356
Bells   Located in downtown Logan, Logan 43138   614-385-4384
Log Cabin   7657 TWP Rd. 234, Logan 43138   614-385-8363
Blackfork Inn   303 N. Water St., Loudonville 44842   419-994-3252
Old Stone House Inn   133 Clemons St., Marblehead 43440   419-798-5922
Folger's Bantam Farm B&B   Rt 6, Mitchell Lane, Marietta 45750   614-374-6919
Oak Hill Bed & Breakfast   16720 Park Rd, Mount Vernon 43050   614-393-2912
Bayberry Inn B&B   25675 St., Rt. 41 N., Peebles 45660   513-587-2221
Centennial House   5995 Center St., Box 67, Peninsula 44264   216-657-2506
Old Island House Inn   102 Madison St., P.O. B, Port Clinton 43452   419-734-2166
Buckeye B&B   P.O. Box 130, Powell 43065   614-548-4555
Le Vent Passant   1539 Langram Rd., Put-In-Bay 43456   419-285-5511
Big Oak   2501 S. Campbell St., Sandusky 44870
Willowtree Inn   1900 W. State Rt. 571, Tipp City 45371   513-667-2957
Mansion View Inn   2035 Collingwood Blvd., Toledo 43620   419-244-5676

Howey House 340 N. Bever St., Wooster 44691 216-264-8231
Worthington Inn 649 High St., Worthington 43085 614-885-2600
Haven @ 4th & Park B&B P.O. Box 467, Zoar 44697 216-874-4672
Weaving Haus P.O. Box 431, Zoar 77697 216-874-3318

West Virginia

BERKELEY SPRINGS

Folkestone B&B	$$ B&B	Full breakfast
Route 2, Box 404, 25411	2 rooms, 1 pb	Sitting room
304-258-3743	C-15+/S-yes/P-no/H-no	hot tub
Hettie Hawvermale		
April 1—November 1		

An English Tudor home in 10 wooded acres, natural country setting. Famous spa baths in town. Rented to one group at a time, 1 to 5 persons.

Highlawn Inn	$$ B&B	Full country breakfast
304 Market Street, 25411	6 rooms, 6 pb	Dinner for groups by res
304-258-5700	Visa, MC	Catering, weddings
Sandra Kauffman	C-no/S-yes/P-no/H-ltd	TV, veranda, porch swing
All year		golf, tennis, hiking

Restored Victorian; luxurious touches, solitude & antiques in quiet mountain town. Minutes from famous mineral baths. Winter Victorian escape packages. Thanksgiving feast.

DAVIS

Bright Morning	$$ EP	Full breakfast $
Rt. 32, William Ave., 26260	●	Restaurant
304-259-2719		Box lunches
Dr. & Mrs. George Bright		

Former lumberjack boarding house in Davis, a small, rural town, renowned for its natural attractions. Historically authentic. A chance to experience a little history & charm.

MARTINSBURG

Boydville Inn @ Martinsburg	$$$ B&B	Full breakfast
601 S. Queen St., 25401	7 rooms, 4 pb	Complimentary wine
304-263-1448	Visa, MC, AmEx ●	Sitting room, music room
Owen Sullivan, Ripley Hotch	French	formal garden
All year		veranda with rockers

Federal mansion furnished with 18th-century antiques on 11 acres near historic sites. Like a visit to an English country house.

MATHIAS

Valley View Farm
Rt. 1, Box 467, 26812
304-897-5229
Ernest & Edna Shipe
All year

$ B&B/AP
4 rooms
C-yes/S-no/P-no/H-no

Full country breakfast
All meals served
Sitting room
library
entertainment

A country hide-away easily accessible to eastern cities. Bountiful meals with homemade breads, sweets, fresh vegetables. Friendly country hospitality.

MIDDLEWAY

Gilbert House B&B
P.O.B. 1104 Rt. 1, 25430
Charlestown
304-725-0637
Jean/Bernie Heiler
All year

$$ B&B
3 rooms, 3 pb
Visa, MC •
C-no/S-ltd/P-no/H-no
German, Spanish

Full gourmet breakfast
Comp tea/wine/champagne
Sitting room, library
piano, fireplaces
walking tour of village

Near Harper's Ferry, magnificent stone house on National Register in 18th-century village. Tasteful antiques, art treasures. Leisurely breakfast. Romantic.

MOOREFIELD

McMechen House Inn
109 N. Main St., 26836
304-538-2417
Art & Evelyn Valloto
exc. 12/24—1/15

$ B&B
6 rooms, 6 pb
Visa, MC, AmEx
C-yes/S-ltd/P-ltd/H-no

Full breakfast
Sitting room
cable TV
A/C

Surrounded by majestic mountains, natural beauty. Built in 1853, furnished in period antiques, emphasis on hospitality and opportunities to see and do.

Countryside, Summit Point, WV

SHEPHERDSTOWN

Thomas Shepherd Inn
P.O. Box 1162, 25443
German & Duke Sts.
304-876-3715
Ed & Carol Ringoot
All year

$$ B&B
6 rooms, 4 pb
Visa, MC
C-12+/S-ltd/P-no/H-no
French, Flemish

Full breakfast
Comp. tea, wine
Living room w/fireplace
bicycles & picnics

1868 restored stately home in quaint historic civil war town. Period antiques, very special breakfasts, fireside beverage, excellent restaurants.

SUMMIT POINT

Countryside
P.O. Box 57, 25446
304-725-2614
Lisa & Daniel Hileman
All year

$ B&B
2 rooms, 2 pb
Visa, MC
C-yes/S-yes/P-yes/H-no

Continental+ to room
Afternoon tea/snack
Sitting room, bicycles
down comforters
feather beds

Near historic Harper's Ferry; quiet & cozy country inn; hiking, cycling, antiquing, sightseeing. For romantic getaways, honeymoons, anniversary & birthday getaway celebrations.

WHEELING

Stratford Springs Inn
355 Oglebay Dr., 26003
304-233-5100
All year

$$$ AP
3 rooms, 3 pb
Visa, MC, AmEx
C-yes/S-yes/H-yes
Spanish, French, Italian

Continental plus,
Lunch & Dinner
Restaurant, bar service
Sitting room, gift shop
tennis courts, pool

Stratford Springs with its gourmet dining, casual atmosphere, period antiques and luxurious lodging rooms, is West Virginia's best-kept secret. . .Only 10 minutes from I-70.

Yesterdays Ltd. B&B
823 Main St., 26003
651, 811 & 817 Main St.
304-232-0864
Bill & Nancy Fields
All year

$$ B&B
12 rooms, 4 pb
Visa, MC
C-yes/S-ltd/P-no/H-no

Full breakfast
Comp. wine, snacks
Sitting room
Whirlpool bath in
some rooms

Lovingly restored Victorian townhouses in historic district overlooking river. Antiques galore. Walk to downtown shopping & events. Perfect getaway or travel stopover.

More Inns. . .

Cabin Lodge   Box 355, Rt. 50, Aurora 26705   304-735-3563
Country Inn   207 So. Washington Str, Berkeley Springs 25411   304-258-2210
Manor   P.O. Box 342, Berkeley Springs 25411   304-258-1552
Shelly's Homestead   Rt.1, Box 1-A, Burlington 26710   304-289-3941
Greenbrier River Inn   Rt. 2, Box 96, Ronceverte, Caldwell 24925   304-647-5652
Carriage Inn   417 E. Washington St., Charles Town 25414   304-728-8003
Cottonwood Inn   Rt. 2, Box 61-S, Charles Town 25414   304-725-3371
Hillbrook Inn   Rt. 2, Box 152, Charles Town 25414   304-725-4223
Pennbrooke Farm B&B   Granny-she Run, Chloe 25235   304-655-7367
Twisted Thistle B&B   P.O. Box 480, Fourth St., Davis 26260   304-259-5389
Cheat River Lodge   Rt. 1, Box 116, Elkins 26241   304-636-2301
Glen Ferris Inn   US Rt. 60, Glen Ferris 25090   304-632-1111
Oak Knoll B&B   Crawley, Greenbrier County 24931   304-392-6903
Fillmore St. B&B   Box 34, Harpers Ferry 25245   301-337-8633
Beekeeper Inn   Helvetia 26224   304-924-6435
The Current B&B   Box 135, Hillsboro 25946   304-653-4722

West Fork Inn   Rt. 2, Box 212, Jane Lew 26378   304-745-4893
Crawford's Country Corner   Box 112, Lost Creek 26385   304-745-3017
Guest House   Low-Gap, Lost River 26811   304-897-5707
The Dunn Country Inn   Rt. 3 Box 33J, Martinsburg 25401   304-263-8646
Hickory Hill Farm   Rt. 1, Box 355, Moorefield 26836   304-538-2511
Maxwell B&B   Rt. 12, Box 197, Morgantown 26505   304-594-3041
Kilmarnock Farms   Rt. 1 Box 91, Orlando 26412   304-452-8319
Bavarian Inn & Lodge   Rt. 1, Box 30, Shepherdstown 25443   304-876-2551
Fuss 'N Feathers   Box 1088, 210 W. German, Shepherdstown 25443   304-876-6469
Little Inn / Yellow Brick Bank   P.O. Box 219, Shepherdstown 25443   304-876-2208
Mecklenberg Inn   128 E. German St, Box 1611, Shepherdstown 25443   304-876-2126
Shang-Ra-La B&B   Rt. 1, Box 156, Shepherdstown 25443   304-876-2391
Morgan Orchard   Rt. 2, Box 114, Sinks Grove 24976   304-772-3638
Cobblestone-on-The-Ohio   103 Charles St., Sistersville 26175   304-652-1206
Wells Inn   316 Charles St., Sistersville 26175   304-652-3111
Elk River Touring Center   Slatyfork 26291   304-572-3771
Garvey House   P.O. Box 98, Winona 25942   304-574-3235

Wisconsin

APPLETON

The Parkside	$$ B&B	Full breakfast
402 E. North St., 54911	1 room, 1 pb	Comp. wine, snacks
414-733-0200	C-no/S-yes/P-no/H-no	Sitting room, library
Bonnie Riley		tennis
All year		TV, A/C

Relax in Old World elegance. Private suite of rooms overlooks lovely city park. Walk to Lawrence University, museum or downtown.

BARABOO

Barrister's House	$ B&B	Continental plus
Box 166, 53913	4 rooms, 4 pb	Comp. wine & beverages
226-9th Ave.	C-6+ /S-no/P-no/H-no	Sitting room, library
608-356-3344		veranda, terrace
Glen & Mary Schulz		screened porch
exc. weekdays Nov.—Apr.		

Colonial charm and simple elegance in a park-like setting. Unique guestrooms, paneled library, fireplaces, screened porch and sitting room with game table and piano.

House of Seven Gables	$$ B&B	Full breakfast
Box 204, 53913	2 rooms, 2 pb	Dining room
215 6th St.	Visa, MC	Victorian gazebo
608-356-8387	C-5+ /S-no/P-no/H-no	piano, A/C
Pam & Ralph Krainik		
All year		

1860 Outstanding Carpenter Gothic Gingerbread House on National Register. Completely furnished in 1860-70 authentic antiques. Featured in publications and on TV's PM Magazine.

BAYFIELD

Cooper Hill House
P.O. Box 1288, 54814
33 S. Sixth St.
715-779-5060
Phil & Sheree Peterson
May—October

$$ B&B
4 rooms, 4 pb
Visa, MC
C-ltd/S-no/P-no/H-no

Continental plus
Sitting room
library
swimming & tennis near

Comfortable historic home in relaxed Lake Superior coastal community. Walking distance to shops, restaurants, waterfront. Sail and explore the Apostle Islands.

Greunke's Inn
17 Rittenhouse, 54814
715-779-5480
Judity Lokken-Strom
April—November

$ EP
7 rooms, 3 pb
Visa, MC
C-yes/S-no/P-no/H-no

Lunch, dinner, beer

Like stepping into one of Norman Rockwell's Saturday Evening Post illustrations—little has changed here since the late 1940's. Old jukebox is a gathering place.

Old Rittenhouse Inn
P.O. Box 584, 54814
301 Rittenhouse Ave.
715-779-5111
Jerry & Mary Phillips
All year

$$ B&B
20 rooms, 20 pb
C-ltd/S-ltd/P-no/H-ltd

Continental plus
Dinner, wine
Bicycles
sitting room
piano, entertainment

Beautiful 30-room Victorian mansion, antiques & 12 working fireplaces. Guests relax on the porch. Overlooks Lake Superior. Also two lovely historic homes.

BELLEVILLE

Abendruh B&B Swiss-style
7019 Gehin Rd., 53508
608-424-3808
Franz & Mathilde Jaggi
All year

$ B&B
3 rooms, 2 pb
Visa, MC •
German, French, Swiss

Full breakfast
Afternoon tea, snacks
Complimentary wine
Sitting room, library
hot tub

True European hospitality. Beautiful, quiet country getaway. Fireplaces, central A/C. Near X-c skiing, biking, nature trails. Many tourist attractions nearby.

CEDARBURG

Stagecoach Inn
W61 N520 Washington Ave., 53012
414-375-0208
Brook & Liz Brown
All year

$$ B&B
12 rooms, 12 pb
Visa, MC, AmEx
C-no/S-no/P-no/H-no

Continental plus
Full bar, restored pub
Library, sitting room
whirlpools
tennis court nearby

Restored 1853 stone inn furnished with antiques and Laura Ashley comforters. Historic pub, chocolate shop and book store on the first floor.

Washington House Inn
W62 N573 Washington Ave., 53012
414-375-3550
Judith I. Drefahl
All year

$$ B&B
29 rooms, 29 pb
•
C-yes/S-yes/P-no/H-yes

Continental plus
Afternoon social
Sitting room, fireplaces
whirlpool baths, sauna
wet bars, bicycles

A country inn in the center of historical district. Breakfast served in charming gathering room. Shopping, golf, winter sports. Whirlpool baths & wet bars in each room.

COLUMBUS

"By the Okeag" | $$ EP | Continental plus
446 Wisconsin St., 53925 | 1 room, 1 pb | Stocked refrigerator
414-623-3007 | Visa, MC | Comp. wine, snacks
Aeton & Bernetta Mather | C-10+ | Private pier with
All year | | canoes and paddle boat

Beautifully decorated guest house by river. Quiet and private, landscaped with flower gardens & gazebo. Private pier with canoe & paddle boat. The perfect spot for relaxation.

ELLISON BAY

Griffin Inn | $$ B&B | Full breakfast
11976 Mink River Rd., 54210 | 10 rooms, 4 pb | Lnch & din. by req.
414-854-4306 | • | Evening popcorn
Laurie & Jim Roberts | C-7+/S-ltd/P-no/H-no | Gathering rooms, library
All year | | bicycles, tennis court

A New England style country inn on the Door County Peninsula, since 1910. Handmade quilts on antique beds. Full country breakfasts. Set on five lovely acres.

EPHRAIM

Eagle Harbor Inn & Cottages | $$ B&B | Continental plus
P.O. Box 72, 54211 | 9 rooms, 9 pb | Sitting rooms
9914 Water St. | Visa, MC • | fireplace room
414-854-2121 | C-15+/H-yes |
Ronald & Barbara Schultz | |
All year | |

An intimate New England styled country inn. Antique-filled; deluxe continental breakfast. Close to boating, beaches, golf course and parks.

Hillside Hotel | $$ B&B/MAP | Full breakfast
P.O. Box 17, 54211 | 12 rooms | 6-course dinner, tea
9980 Water St. | Visa, MC, AmEx, Disc • | Full service restaurant
414-854-2417/800-423-7023 | C-yes/S-no/P-no/H-no | Private beach, mooring
David & Karen McNeil | | charcoaler for picnics
May—Nov 1, Jan—Feb | |

Country-Victorian hotel with harbor view, private beach, specialty breakfasts, gourmet dinners, original furnishings, spectacular views; near galleries, shops; in resort area.

FISH CREEK

Thorp House Inn | $ B&B | Continental plus
P.O. Box 90, 54212 | 4 rooms | Sitting room w/fireplace
4135 Bluff Rd. | Norwegian | library
414-868-2444 | | bicycles
C. & S. Falck-Pedersen | |
All year | |

Antique-filled historic home backed by wooded bluff, overlooking bay. Walk to beach, park, shops and restaurants. Winter: cross-country skiing.

White Gull Inn | $ | Full breakfast
Box 175, 54212 | 16 rooms, 9 pb | Lunch, dinner
414-868-3517 | C-yes/S-yes/P-no/H-ltd | Bicycles
Andy & Jon Coulson | | entertainment
all year | | piano

Situated between the bluff and the bay in Fish Creek on Wisconsin's Door Peninsula; charming turn-of-the-century inn.

HARTLAND

Monches Mill House	$$ B&B	Continental plus
W301 N9430 Hwy E, 53029	4 rooms, 2 pb	Complimentary wine
414-966-7546	C-yes/S-yes/P-yes/H-yes	Sitting room
Elaine Taylor	French	hot tub, bicycles
May—December		tennis, canoeing

House built in 1842, located on the bank of the mill pond, furnished in antiques, choice of patio, porch or gallery for breakfast enjoyment.

HUDSON

Jefferson-Day House	$$ B&B	Full breakfast
1109-3rd St., 54016	4 rooms, 2 pb	Snacks
715-386-7111	•	Sitting room
The Millers	C-yes/H-yes	library
All year	Spanish	

1857 home just blocks away from beautiful St. Croix River. Skiing nearby. 15 minutes from St. Paul/Minneapolis. Antique collections. Three-course full breakfast.

JANESVILLE

Jackson Street Inn B&B	$ B&B	Full breakfast
210 S. Jackson St., 53545	4 rooms, 2 pb	Comp. tea, wine
608-754-7250	Visa, MC •	Sitting room, library
Ilah & Bob Sessler	C-yes/S-yes/P-no/H-no	fireplace, shuffleboard
All year		cable TV, putting green

Near I-90, home has spacious rooms, Old World charm. Full gourmet breakfast. Great golf, bike, ski trails. Brochure available.

KENOSHA

Manor House	$$$ B&B	Continental breakfast
6536 3rd Avenue, 5314	4 rooms, 4 pb	Meals on arrangement
414-658-0014	Visa, MC •	Complimentary wine
Ron & Mary Rzeplinski	C-12+/S-ltd/P-no/H-no	Sitting room, library
All year	French	piano, bicycles

Georgian mansion overlooking Lake Michigan. Furnished with 18th-century antiques. Formal landscaped grounds. Midway—Chicago & Milwaukee. National Register.

LAKE GENEVA-White water

Greene House B&B	$ B&B	Full breakfast
RR2, Box 214, Hwy 12, 53190	5 rooms	Dinner by res.
414-495-8771	AmEx •	Sitting room, library
Lynn & Mayner Greene	C-6+/S-ltd/P-no/H-no	catering, shop
All year		wine tasting

1840's farmhouse filled with country charm, Kettle Morraine recreational activities abound. Unique shopping in our Hayloft, gourmet meals our specialty.

MADISON

Collins House B&B	$$ B&B	Full breakfast (wkends)
704 E. Gorham St., 53703	4 rooms, 4 pb	Cont. breakfast (wkdays)
608-255-4230	Visa, MC	Comp. chocolate truffles
Barbara & Mike Pratzel	C-yes/S-ltd/P-yes/H-no	Sitting room w/fireplace
All year		library, movies on video

Restored prairie school style. Overlooks Lake Mendota, near university and state capitol. Elegant rooms, wonderful gourmet breakfasts and pastries.

Hill House B&B	$$ B&B	Full breakfast
2117 Sheridan Dr., 53704	3 rooms, 1 pb	Snacks
608-244-2224	•	Library, tennis courts
Anne & Larry Stuart	C-yes/S-ltd/P-ltd/H-no	fishing, jogging, hiking
All year		boat rentals, x-c skiing

Beautiful country garden setting in the city, complete with romantic gazebo. Full recreational facilities. 10 min. to downtown and campus. Full breakfast every day. Enjoy!

Plough Inn B&B	$ B&B	Continental+ (wkday)
3402 Monroe St., 53711	3 rooms, 3 pb	Full breakfast (wkend)
608-238-2981	Visa, MC	Complimentary wine
R. Ganser & K. Naherny	C-no/S-no/P-no/H-no	Sitting room
All year		new "tap" room added

Historic 1850's inn with 3 charming, spacious rooms. Arborview room has fireplace and whirlpool bath. Across from Arboretum, near university campus.

MINERAL POINT

Chesterfield Inn	$ B&B	Continental plus
20 Commerce St., 53565	8 rooms	Lunch, dinner
608-987-3682	Visa, MC	Restaurant, bar service
V. Duane Rath	C-yes/S-yes/P-yes/H-no	Garden terrace
All year		bicycles

Historic stone stagecoach inn in Cornish settlement. Charming outdoor dining with weekend entertainment. Plenty to do including antiquing, cycling, theater.

ONTARIO

Inn at Wildcat Mountain	$ B&B	Full breakfast
P.O. Box 112, 54651	3 rooms	Snacks, comp. wine
Hwy 33	Visa, MC, AmEx	Parlor, library
608-337-4352	C-10+/P-ltd	patio, spacious porches
Patricia & Wendell Barnes		5 acres of grounds
All year		

Lovely 1910 Greek Revival home along Kickapoo River in Wisconsin's Hidden Valleys. . .at the entrance to Wildcat Mountain State Park & Amish Country. "Wonderful" full breakfasts.

OSHKOSH

Tiffany Inn	$ B&B	Continental plus
206 Algoma Blvd, 54901	12 rooms, 12 pb	Library, sitting room
414-426-1000	Visa, MC	living room w/fireplace
Linda Anderson	C-no/S-yes/P-no/H-yes	games, books
All year		

Beautifully appointed rooms will help you step back in time. Close to downtown, the University of Wisconsin, the grand opera house, the museum and shopping.

POYNETTE

Jamieson House	$$ B&B	Full breakfast
P.O. Box 829, 53955	10 rooms, 10 pb	Restaurant, bar
407 N. Franklin St.	AmEx, DC	Garden room
608-635-4100	C-ltd/S-ltd/P-ltd/H-no	piano, bicycles
James/Carole Gacek		
All year		

The Jamieson House features intimate gourmet dining amid quiet Victorian elegance. Guest rooms have sumptuous velvet couches, sunken baths, antiques.

Chesterfield Inn, Mineral Point, WI

SISTER BAY

Renaissance Inn
414 Maple Dr., 54234
414-854-5107
John & Jodee Faller
May-November, January-March

$$ B&B
5 rooms, 5 pb
Visa, MC, AmEx
C-no/S-yes/P-no/H-no

Full breakfast
Lunch, dinner
Restaurant
Snacks
Sitting room

Turn-of-the-century inn boasts chef as its host and an elegant Creole dining room. Snug, pleasant rooms.

SPARTA

Franklin Victorian
220 E. Franklin St., 54656
608-269-3894
Jane & Llyod Larson
All year

$$ B&B
4 rooms
C-10+

Full breakfast
Afternoon tea, snacks
Sitting room
library
canoe rental

Relax in quiet, gracious comfort—spacious rooms, fine woods. Delectable breakfasts. Surrounding area abounds with beauty. Recreation all four seasons.

Just-N-Trails B&B
Route 1, Box 263, 54656
608-269-4522
Don & Donna Justin
All year

$$ B&B
3 rooms
Visa, MC •
C-yes/S-no/P-no/H-no

Full breakfast
Log cabin available
bicycles
hiking trails
X-c ski trails

Roam on a 200-acre dairy farm, daydream by a pond. Ride on nearby Elroy-Sparta bike trail, cross-country ski our 20 K of trails. Relax in our charming country home.

STURGEON BAY ─────────────────

Gray Goose B&B	$$ B&B	Full breakfast
4258 Bay Shore Dr., 54235	4 rooms	Snacks
414-743-9100	Visa, MC, AmEx	Sitting room, library
Jack & Jessie Burkhardt	S-ltd	full covered porch
All year		cable TV, games

Comfortable Civil War home; genuine antiques. Quiet, wooded setting north of city. Wooded view. Full country breakfasts and personal attention.

Inn at Cedar Crossing	$$ B&B	Full breakfst (wint/spr)
336 Louisiana St., 54235	9 rooms, 9 pb	Cont. plus (summer/fall)
414-743-4200	Visa, MC, DC	Snacks, restaurant
Terry Wulf	C-6+/S-ltd/P-no/H-no	Sitting room
All year		whirlpools

1884 inn is situated in historic district close to shops, restaurants, museum, beaches. Country antique decor, fireplaces, whirlpools, common room.

White Lace Inn	$$ B&B	Continental plus
16 N. 5th Ave., 54235	15 rooms, 15 pb	Tea, coffee, chocolate
414-743-1105	Visa, MC •	Sitting room
Bonnie & Dennis Statz	C-no/S-ltd/P-no/H-ltd	tandem bicycles
All year		

A Victorian country inn with romantic decor; 15 charming guest rooms, all with fine antiques, authentic Victorian or poster bed; 10 w/fireplace, 7 w/whirlpool and fireplace.

VIROQUA ─────────────────

Viroqua Heritage Inn	$ B&B	Full breakfast
220 E. Jefferson St., 54665	4 rooms	Baby grand piano
608-637-3306	Visa, MC •	mystery weekends
Nancy L. Rhodes	C-yes/S-ltd/P-no/H-no	near skiing, golf, hiking
All year		

Elegant Victorian home, lovingly restored by your innkeeper, offers a peaceful and romantic sojourn. Abundant breakfast served. Near sports, sightseeing.

More Inns. . .

Gallery House   **215** No. Main St., Alma 54610   608-685-4975
Laue House Inn   **Box** 176, Alma 54610   608-685-4923
Pinehurst Inn   Hwy 13, P.O. Box 222, Bayfield 54814   715-779-3676
Ty-Bach   2817, Beloit 53511   608-365-1039
Willson House   320 Superior St., Chippewa Falls 54729   715-723-0055
Son Ne Vale Farm B&B   Rt 1 Box 132, Colfax 54730   715-962-4342
Creamery   Box 22, Downsville 54735   715-664-8354
Greystone Farms   770 Adam's Rd., East Troy 53120   414-495-8485
Country Gardens B&B   6421 Hwy. 42, Egg Harbor 54209   414-743-7434
Griffin Inn   11976 Mink River Rd., Ellison Bay 54210   414-854-4306
Proud Mary   P.O. Box 193, Fish Creek 54212   414-868-3442
Whistling Swan Inn   P.O. Box 193, Main St., Fish Creek 54212   414-868-3442
Strawberry Hill   Rte.1, Box 524-D, Greenlake 54941   414-294-3450
McConnell Inn   497 S. Lawson Dr.,Box 639, Greenlake 54941   414-294-6430
Mustard Seed   205 California, Box 262, Hayward 54843   715-634-2908
Wisc. House Stagecoach Inn   2105 East Main, Hazel Green 53811   608-854-2233

Sandy Scott   1520 State St., La Crosse 54601   608-784-7145
Trillium   Rte.2, Box 121, La Farge 54639   608-625-4492
Chateau Madeleine   P.O. Box 27, La Pointe 54850   715-747-2463
OJ's Victorian Village   P.O. Box 98, Hwy 12, Lake Delton 53940   608-254-6568
Eleven Gables Inn on Lake   493 Wrigley Dr., Lake Geneva 53147   414-248-8393
Elizabethian Inn   463 Wrigley Dr., Lake Geneva 53147   414-248-9131
Seven Pines Lodge   Lewis 54851   715-653-2323
Oak Hill Farm   9850 Highway 80, Livingston 53554   608-943-6006
Mansion Hill Inn   424 N. Pinckneg St., Madison 53703   608-255-3999
Lauerman Guest House Inn   1975 Riverside Ave., Marinette 54143
Ogden House   2237 No. Lake Dr., Milwaukee 53202   414-272-2740
Pfister Hotel   424 East Wisconsin Ave., Milwaukee 53202   414-273-8222
Duke House B&B   618 Maiden St., Mineral Point 53565   608-987-2821
Wilson House Inn   110 Dodge St., Mineral Point 53565   608-987-3600
Wm. A. Jones House   215 Ridge St. (Hwy 151), Mineral Point 53565   608-987-2337
Inn   30 Wisconsin Ave., Montreal 54550   715-561-5180
Rambling Hills Tree Farm B&B   8825 Willever Lane, Newton 53063   414-726-4388
Marybrooke Inn   705 W. New York Ave., Oshkosh 54901   414-426-4761
Halfway House B&B   Rt. 2, Box 80, Oxford 53952   608-586-5489
Limberlost Inn   2483 Hwy 17, Phelps 54554   715-545-2685
52 Stafford (Irish Guest House)   P.O. Box 217, Plymouth 53073   414-893-0552
Breese Waye B&B   816 Macfarlane Rd., Portage 53901   608-742-5281
Country Aire   Rt. 2 Box 175, Portage 53901   608-742-5716
Mansion   323 S. Central, Richland Center 53581   608-647-2808
Victorian Swan on Water   1716 Water St., Stevens Point 54481   715-345-0595
Lake House   RR 2, Box 217, Strum 54770   715-695-3519
Bay Shore Inn   4205 Bay Shore Dr., Sturgeon Bay 54235   414-743-4551
Gandt's Haus und Hof   2962 Lake Forest Park Rd, Sturgeon Bay 54235   414-743-1238
The Nautical Inn   234 Kentucky St., Sturgeon Bay 54235
Serendipity Farm   Rt. 3 Box 162, Viroqua 54665   608-637-7708
Rosenberry Inn   511 Franklin St., Wausau 54401   715-842-5733
Westby House   State St., Westby 54667   608-634-4112
Foxmoor B&B   Fox River Rd., Wilmot 53192   414-862-6161
Bennett House   825 Oak St., Wisconsin Dells 53965   608-254-2500
House on River Rd.   922 River Rd., Wisconsin Dells 53965   608-253-5573
Sherman House   930 River Rd., Box 397, Wisconsin Dells 53965   608-253-2721

Alberta

Brewster's Kananaskis Guest Ranch
General Delivery, T0L 1X0
403-673-3737
The Brewster Family
May 1—October 15

$$ B&B
27 rooms, 27 pb
Visa, MC •
C-yes/S-yes/P-no/H-yes

Full breakfast
Lic. dining room, lounge
Seminar facility, golf
whirlpool, horses
Western BBQ's

Turn-of-the-century guest ranch; private cabins and chalet units; antique furniture. Operated by 5th-generation Brewsters. 45 mi. west of Calgary, 30 mi east of Banff.

More Inns...

Crazee Akerz Farm   RR #1, Bentley T0C 0J0   403-843-6444
Nordbye House   4801 49 St., Camrose T4V 1M8   403-672-8131
Cougar Creek Inn   P.O.Box 1162, Canmore T0L 0M0   403-678-4751
Haus Alpenrose Lodge   629 9th St., Box 723, Canmore T0L 0M0   403-678-4134
C.A. McMillan's   512 54th Ave. W., Clausholm T0L 0T0
Edmonton Hostel   10422 91st St., Edmonton   403-429-0140
Back Porch B&B   266 Northumberland St., Fredericton E3B 3J6   506-454-6875
Gwynalta Farm   Gwynne T0C 1L0   403-352-3587
Harbour House   Box 54, #1 Lakeshore Dr., Hay River X0E 0R0   403-874-2233
Black Cat Guest Ranch   Box 976, Hinton T0E 1B0   403-865-3084
Mesa Creek Ranch Vacation   General Delivery, Millarville T0L 1K0   403-931-3573
Broadview Farm   RR #2, Millet T0C 1Z0   403-387-4963
Timber Ridge Homestead   Box 94, Nanton T0L 1R0   403-646-5683
Wildflower Country House   Box 8, Site 1, R.R.2, Okotoks T0L 1T0
Rafter Six Ranch Resort   Seebe T0L 1X0   403-673-3622

British Columbia

CAMPBELL RIVER

April Point Lodge
P.O. Box 1, V9W 4Z9
April Pt. Rd., Quadra Isl
604-285-2222
Eric Peterson
April 15—October 15

$$$ EP
36 rooms, 42 pb
Major credit cards ●
C-yes/S-yes/P-ltd/H-ltd
Fr., Rus., Ger., Japan.

Full breakfast
Restaurant, bar
Sitting room, piano
entertainment (summer)
saltwater pool

Personal service is our pride. More than one staff member per guest. Saltwater pool, many languages spoken. One to five bedroom deluxe guest houses.

Campbell River Lodge
1760 Island Hwy., V9W 2E7
604-287-7446/800-663-7212
Ted Arbour
All year

$ B&B
30 rooms, 30 pb
Visa, MC, EnRoute ●
C-yes/S-yes/P-small/H-no

Continental breakfast
Lunch, dinner, pub
Whirlpool, sauna
laundry, phones

The BIG little fishing resort on the famous Campbell River. Restaurant and pub, racquets. Very experienced saltwater salmon and freshwater guides. Est. 1948.

FORT STEELE

Wild Horse Farm
Box 7, V0B 1N0
604-426-6000
Bob/Orma Termuende
May—October

$$ B&B
3 rooms, 3 pb
●
C-no/S-ltd/P-ltd/H-no

Full homebaked breakfast
Sitting room
standard & player pianos

Spacious early-1900's log-faced country manor nestled in the Rocky Mountains; extensive lawns, gardens, trees on grounds. Across from Fort Steele Historic Park.

GABRIOLA ISLAND

Surf Lodge Ltd.
RR1, Site 1, V0R 1X0
Berry Point Rd.
604-247-9231
David & Margaret Halliday
May—October

$ EP
18 rooms, 18 pb
Visa, MC ●
C-4+/S-yes/P-no/H-ltd

Tea, dinner, bar
Sitting room, piano
swimming pool
tennis courts, bicycles

Situated on 15 acres by the shores of the Straits of Georgia. Incomparable sunsets. Nine-hole golf course nearby.

HORNBY ISLAND

Sea Breeze Lodge
V0R 1Z0
604-335-2321
Brian & Gail Bishop
All year; AP 6/15—9/15

$$ AP
11 rooms, 11 pb
1
C-yes/S-yes/P-yes/H-ltd
Spanish

Full breakfast
All homecooked meals
Sitting room, piano
grass tennis courts
hot tub, fishing guide

Sea Breeze Lodge—mentioned in '83 edition of West World. Near the ocean. Breakfast, home made pastries.

KLEENA KLEENE

Chilanko Lodge & Resort	$$$ B&B	Full breakfast
Gen. Del., Hwy 20, V0L 1M0	14 rooms, 7 pb	Lunch, dinner
604-Kleena K	Visa, MC ●	Sitting room, library
Mark Sudweeks	C-yes/S-yes/P-yes/H-yes	hot tub, sauna, lake
All year		airstrip, horses

Pristine lakefront wilderness resort—wildlife abounds—world class fishing—amenities unmatched—beach—unparalleled professional staff—satisfaction guaranteed.

MAYNE ISLAND

Gingerbread House	B&B	Full breakfast
Campbell Bay Rd., V0N 2J0	4 rooms, 2 pb	Fine dining by arrgmnt
604-539-3133	Visa, MC ●	Sitting room, library
Ken Someroille	C-12+	bicycles, tennis courts
March 1—October 31		moorage & docking avail.

Completely restored heritage home (circa 1900). Antique-filled, color coordinated guest rooms emphasize comfort & elegance. Secluded setting, striking mountain & ocean views.

MILL BAY

Pinelodge Farm B&B	$$ B&B	Full farm breakfast
3191 Mutter Rd., V0R 2P0	7 rooms, 7 pb	Sitting room
604-743-4083	C-yes/S-ltd/P-no/H-no	museum
Cliff & Barbara Clarke		antique sales
All year		

Our lodge is on a 30-acre farm with panoramic ocean views. Each room is furnished with exquisite antiques and stained glass windows. Museum open to public. Antique sales.

NANOOSE BAY

The Lookout	$$ B&B	Full breakfast
Box 71, Blueback Dr, V0R 2R0	3 rooms, 2 pb	Sitting room
RR 2, 3381 Dolphin Dr.	●	library
604-468-9796	C-7+	fishing charter avail.
Marj & Herb Wilkie	Australian, American	golf course nearby
May—September		

Spectacular views of Georgia Strait, watch boats, eagles, cruise ships, maybe even Orca whales. Country breakfast on wraparound deck. Golf, fishing, marina nearby. Quiet.

NORTH VANCOUVER

Grouse Mountain B&B	$$ B&B	Full gourmet breakfast
900 Clements Ave., V7R 2K7	2 rooms, 1 pb	Sitting room
604-986-9630	●	piano
Lyne & John Armstrong	C-yes/S-no/P-yes/H-no	
All year	French, German	

Nestled in the foothills of Grouse Mountain, our comfortable, modern home awaits you. Features include large private rooms, warm hospitality.

Helen's B&B	$$ B&B	Full breakfast
302 E. 5th St., V7L 1L1	2 rooms, 2 pb	Sitting room
604-985-4869	●	game room
Helen Boire	C-yes/S-ltd/P-no/H-no	
All year	French	

Lovely, comfortable Victorian home. Views to ocean and city. Only five blocks to sea. Near all transport and attractions. Grouse Mountain skiing nearby.

Beaconsfield Inn, Victoria, B.C

Platt's B&B
4393 Quinton Pl., V7R 4A8
604-987-4100
Nancy/Elwood Platt
All year

$ B&B
2 rooms, 1 pb
●
C-no/S-no/P-no/H-no
English

Full breakfast

Quiet park-like area, homemade bread and jams. 15 minutes to heart of town and our famous Stanley Park.

Sue's Victorian B&B
152 E. 3rd, V7L 1E6
604-985-1523
Sue Chalmers
All year

$ EP/B&B
2 rooms, 1 pb
●
C-yes/S-no/P-no/H-no
English

Cont. & Full breakfast
Kitchen privileges
Piano, laundry
guest parking
babysitting by arrgmnt

Lovely restored 1909 home has gorgeous harbor view, individually keyed rooms, centrally located for transportation, shopping, restaurants and tourist attractions.

PARSON ——————————————————————————————

Taliesin Guest House B&B
Box 101, V0A 1LO
Spence off Beard's Creek
604-348-2247
M. & B. Kelly-McArthur
All year

$ B&B
3 rooms
Visa ●
C-yes/S-no/P-no/H-no
Some French, German

Full breakfast
Lunch, dinner served
Library
sitting room

Nestled in the Rocky Mountains, close to major National Parks, our modern log home offers spectacular views, seclusion and serenity in nature.

PENDER ISLAND

Corbett House B&B	$$ B&B	Full breakfast
Corbett Rd., V0N 2M0	3 rooms, 3 pb	Dinner by res., aft. tea
604-629-6305	Visa, MC	Sitting room, library
Linda Wolfe/John Eckfeldt	C-no/S-no/P-no/H-no	bicycles, canoe/kayak
All year	English, French, Spanish	fishing, golf nearby

Charming restored heritage farmhouse in the Gulf Islands. Quiet rural setting; close to ocean & ferry. Fine dining by reservation, eclectic library and music of your choice.

SALMON ARM

Silver Creek Guest House	$ B&B	Full breakfast
6820-30th Ave. SW, V1E 4M1	4 rooms	Afternoon tea
604-832-8870	Visa, MC, AmEx	Sitting room
Gisela Bodnar	C-yes/S-ltd/P-ltd/H-yes	bicycles
All year	German	

Charming log house with beautiful scenery. Surrounded by mountains, 5 minutes to Shuswap Lake with crystal-clear water for swimming, boating and fishing.

SOOKE

Sooke Harbour House	$$$ B&B	Full breakfast
1528 Whiffen Spit Rd.	15 rooms, 15 pb	Light buffet lunch incl.
RR #4, V0S 1N0	Visa, MC, AmEx, DC •	Dinner, bar, entertnmnt.
604-642-3421/604-642-4944	C-yes/S-ltd/P-yes/H-yes	Sitting room, piano
Fredrica & Sinclair Philip	French	jacuzzi, bikes, hot tubs
All year		

Charmingly furnished oceanview guestrooms. Outstanding imaginative gourmet restaurant serves local sea, land produce. Guests say the inn is romantic, relaxing, magical, memorable.

VANCOUVER

Diana Luxury Home B&B	$$ B&B	Full breakfast
1019 E. 38th Ave., V5W 1J4	8 rooms, 2 pb	Jacuzzi, garden
604-321-2855/604-325-2335	•	sitting room, patio
Diana Piwko	C-no/S-yes/P-yes/H-yes	babysitting avail.
All year	Polish,Russ,Yugos,Czech	TV, games, bicycles

Luxury home in a central area. Free airport pickup. Comfortable, friendly atmosphere. Accommodation right in downtown Vancouver also available.

Rose Garden Guest House	$ B&B	Full breakfast
6808 Dawson St., V5S 2W3	2 rooms	Afternoon tea, snacks
604-435-7129	MC •	Sitting room
Dwyla & Ed Beglaw	C-yes	
All year		

Warm hospitality, Canadian style. Eiderdown quilts, rose decor, TV, comp. snacks. Close to gardens, golf, downtown. Wholesome home baking every morning; vegetarian food avail.

Vincent's Guest House	$ B&B	Full breakfast
1741 Grant St., V5L 2Y6	6 rooms	Sitting room
604-254-7462	•	TV, stereo, washer/dryer
All year	S-yes	bicycles
	Fr, Ital, Sp, Germ, Port	bus or airport pickup

Guest house, hostel style. International atmosphere; meet a lot of travelers, young and old. Excellent location; only 1 mile from downtown. Generous hospitality.

West End Guest House
1362 Haro St., V6E 1G2
604-681-2889
C. Weigom/G. Christie
All year

$$ B&B
7 rooms, 7 pb
Visa, MC •
C-no/S-no/P-no/H-no
English, French

Full breakfast
Sitting room, library
parking, TV in lounge
piano, phones in rooms

Walk to Stanley Park, beaches, Robson Street shops and restaurants; then enjoy the quiet ambiance of our comfortable historic inn.

VERNON

Twin Willows By The Lake
Site 10, Comp 16, RR 4,
7456 Kennedy Ln., V1T 6L7
604-542-8293
Colleen & Rod Pringle
May—October

$$ B&B
2 rooms, 1 pb
C-yes/S-no/P-yes/H-no
French, German, Spanish

Full breakfast
Library, lake
sailboat hire
wharf, swimming

Spacious lakefront suite (bath & entrance) in sunny Okanagan. Every window lakeview. Peaceful, private. Friendly hosts, delicious good. Swimming, moorage, hammock. Can sleep 6.

VICTORIA

Abigail's
906 McClure St., V8V 3E7
604-388-5363
Catherine Challinor
All year

$$ B&B
16 rooms, 16 pb
Visa, MC •
C-yes

Full breakfast
Complimentary sherry
Library
sitting room
bicycles

Completely updated classic Tudor building. Private jacuzzi tubs, fireplaces and goose down comforters. Walk to downtown. Delicious breakfast. First-class smiling hospitality.

Battery Street Guest House
670 Battery St., V8V 1E5
604-385-4632
Pamela Verduyn
All year

$ B&B
6 rooms, 2 pb
C-ltd/S-no/P-no/H-no
Dutch

Continental plus
Sitting room

Comfortable guesthouse (1898) in downtown Victoria. Centrally located; walk to town, sites, Beacon Hill Park & ocean. Ample breakfast. Host speaks Dutch as a first language.

Beaconsfield Inn
998 Humboldt St., V8V 2Z8
604-384-4044
Christine Kirkham
All year

$$$ B&B
12 rooms, 12 pb
Visa, MC •
C-yes/S-ltd

Full breakfast
Complimentary sherry
Sun room, library
piano
bicycles

Award-winning restoration of an English mansion. Walk to downtown. Antiques throughout; rich textures, velvets, leather, warm woods. Delicious breakfast. Pampering service.

Captain's Palace Inn & Rest.
309 Belleville St., V8V 1X2
604-388-9191
F. Prior, H. Beirnes
All year

$$$ B&B
14 rooms, 14 pb
Visa, MC, AmEx •
C-no/S-no/P-no/H-no

Full breakfast
Complimentary wine

1897 mansion with crystal chandeliers, stained glass, antiques and restaurant; near heart of Victoria; full view of Inner Harbor; Christmas shop & chocolate factory to visit.

Elk Lake Lodge
5259 Patricia Bay Hwy. 17,
V8Y 1S8
604-658-8879
Brenda & Ken Hicks
All year

$$ B&B
4 rooms, 2 pb
Visa, MC
C-yes/S-ltd/P-ltd/H-no
French, Spanish

Full breakfast
Afternoon tea
Library
sitting room

Formerly a unique 1910 monastery and church. Antique furnishings with bedrooms and living room overlooking Elk Lake. Ten minutes from the city center, ferries.

Hibernia B&B
747 Helvetia Cr., V8Y 1M1
604-658-5519
Aideen Lydon
All year

$ B&B
3 rooms
MC •
C-yes
French, Spanish, Gaelic

Full breakfast
Sitting room
large lawn with trees
vines

Peaceful. 15 minutes from Victoria, ferries, airport, Butchart Gardens, cul-de-sac; 5 minutes off Highway 17. Full Irish breakfast. Antique furnishings.

Sunnymeade House Inn
1002 Fenn Ave., V8Y 1P3
604-658-1414
Jack & Nancy Thompson
All year

$$ B&B
5 rooms, 1 pb
Visa, MC

Full or Cont. breakfast
Restaurant, bar service
Afternoon tea
Sitting room
tennis courts

Village by the Sea— Walk to shops, restaurants, beach. Country-style B&B inn. Beautiful decor & furnishings. Sumptuous full breakfast.

Top o' Triangle Mountain
3442 Karger Terr., V9C 3K5
604-478-7853
Henry & Pat Hansen
All year

$$ B&B
3 rooms, 3 pb
Visa, MC •
C-yes/S-ltd/P-no/H-yes
Danish

Full breakfast
Sitting room

Warm, solid cedar home tucked in among the firs. Breathtaking view. Clean, comfortable beds. Hospitality and good food are our specialties. One two-room suite available.

Tucker's B&B
5373 Pat Bay Hwy. 17, V8Y 1S9
604-658-8404/604-658-5531
Michele & Ian MacDonald
All year

$ B&B
4 rooms, 2 pb
Visa, MC •
C-yes/S-ltd/P-no/H-no
French

Full breakfast
Afternoon tea, snacks
Restaurants nearby
Sitting room, parlour
bicycles, piano

Country-style B&B; lakeside with swimming, parks and windsurfing; hearty home cooking; character rooms; close to Butchart Gardens and downtown Victoria.

More Inns. . .

Aguilar House   Bamfield V0R 1B0   604-728-3323
Bobbing Boats   Box 88, 7212 Peden Ln., Brentwood Bay V0S 1A0   604-652-9828
Brentwood Bay B&B   Box 403, Brentwood Bay V0S 1A0   604-652-2012
Dogwoods   302 Birch St., Campbell River V9W 2S6   604-287-4213
Grants   RR 1, Chemainns V0R 1K0   604-246-3768
Dahlia Patch   3675 Minto Rd., Courtenay V9N 5M8
Wilcuma Resort   RR 3, Cobble Hill V0R 1L0   604-748-8737

Denman Is. Guest House   Box 9, Denman Rd., Denman Island V0R 1T0   604-335-2688
Fairburn Farm   RR 7, Duncan V9L 4W4   604-746-4637
Bradshaw's Minac Lodge   On Canim Lake, Eagle Creek V0K 1L0   604-397-2416
Gimmy's Farm/Guesthouse   SS2, Site 13, Comp. 11, Fort St. John V1J 4M7   604-787-9104
Lynn's Lodge   Box 253, Endarko Mine Rd, Fraser Lake V0J 1S0   604-699-6670
Hummingbird Inn   Sturdies Bay Rd., Galiano Island V0N 1P0   604-539-5472
La Berengerie   Montague Harbor Bl., Galiano Island V0N 1P0   604-539-5392
Mountain View Lodge   P.O. Box 90, Glendale Springs 28629   919-982-2233
Lord Jim's Resort Hotel   RR #1, Ole's Cove Rd., Halfmoon Bay V0N 1Y0   604-885-7038
Blair House   1299 Rodondo Place, Kelowna V1V 1G6   604-762-5090
The Cat's Meow   5299 Chute Lake Rd., Kelowna V1Y 7R3   604-764-7407
Gables Country Inn   2405 Bering Rd. Box 1153, Kelowna V1Y 7P8   604-768-4468
Manana Lodge   Box 9 RR 1, Ladysmith V0R 2E0   604-245-2312
Yellow Point Lodge   RR 3, Ladysmith V0R 2E0   604-245-7422
Fernhill Lodge   Box 140, Mayne Island V0N 2J0   604-539-2544
Heritage Inn   422 Vernon St., Nelson   604-352-5331
B&B for Visitors   10356 Skagit Dr., North Delta V4C 2K9   604-588-8866
Katie's B&B   217 Keith Rd., No. Vancouver V7L 1V4   604-987-1092
Laburnum Cottage   1388 Terrace Ave., No. Vancouver V7R 1B4   604-988-4877
West Coast Contemporary   RR1, Site 116 C71, Parksville V0R 2S0   604-248-2585
Rose Cottage   1362 Naish Dr., Penticton V2A 3B6   604-492-3462
Tina's Tuc-Inn   158 Steward Place, Penticton V2A 3Y9   604-492-3366
Feathered Paddle B&B   7 Queesto Dr., Port Renfrew V0S 1K0   604-647-5433
Quilchena Hotel   Quilchena V0E 2R0   604-378-2611
Ram's Head Inn   Red Mt. Ski Area Box 636, Rossland V0G 1Y0   604-362-9577
Cindosa B&B   3951 40th St. NE, Salmon Arm V1E 4M4   604-832-3342
Hastings House   Box 1110, Ganges, Salt Spring Island V0S 1E0   800-661-9255
Fen Mor Manor   Box 453, Sicamous V0E 2V0   604-836-4994
Three Pines Lodge   Si.85,RR#2, 5113 Caldwell, Summerland V0H 1Z0   604-494-1661
Hirsch's Place   10336-145 A St., Surrey V3R 3S1   604-588-3326
Clayoquot Lodge   P.O. Box 188, Tofino V0R 2Z0   604-725-3284
Burley's Lodge   Box 193, Ucluelet V0R 3A0   604-726-4444
Lola's Bed&B   2036 Stephens St., Vancouver V6K 3W1   604-733-7321
"The Cabin"   7603 Westkal Rd., Vernon V1B 1Y4   000-542-3021
Five Junipers   3704 24th Ave., Vernon V1T 1L9   604-549-3615
Schroth Farm   Site 6, Comp 25, R.R.8, Vernon V1T 8L6   604-545-0010
Windmill House B&B   5672 Learmouth Rd., Vernon V1T 6L4   000-549-2804
Camelot   P.O. Box 5038, Stn. B, Victoria V8R 6N3   604-592-8589
Cherry Bank Hotel   825 Burdetl Ave., Victoria V8W 1B3
Craigmyle Bed & Breakfast   1037 Craigdorroch Rd., Victoria V8S 2A5   604-595-5411
Oak Bay Guest House   1052 Newport Ave., Victoria V8S 5E3   604-598-3812
Olde England Inn   429 Lampson St., Victoria   604-388-4353
Oxford Castle Inn   133 George Rd., East, Victoria V9A 1L1   604-388-6431
Portage Inlet B&B   993 Portage Rd., Victoria V8Z 1K9   604-479-4594
Rose Cottage B&B   3059 Washington Ave., Victoria V8A 1P7   604-381-5985
Heritage House B&B   1100 Burnside Rd., W. Victoria V8Z 1N3   604-479-0892
Margit's Mountain Retreat   Box 466, Whistler V0N 1B0   604-932-5974
Sabey House   Box 341, Whistler V0N 1B0   604-932-3498
Hotel   129 W. Third St., Winona 55987   507-452-5460

Manitoba

MORRIS

Deerbank Farm
Box 23, RR 2, R0G 1K0
204-746-8395
Kathleen Jorgenson
All year

$ B&B
3 rooms
C-yes/S-ltd/P-ask/H-no

Full breakfast
Supper by request
Complimentary tea
Sitting room, piano
bicycles, pool table

Working farm with extra animals for our guests. In heart of the Red River Valley, one hour to Winnipeg.

TREHERNE

Beulah Land
Box 26, R0G 2V0
204-723-2828
Wilf. Eadie
All year

$ B&B
3 rooms
C-yes/S-yes/P-no/H-no

Full breakfast
All meals
Hot tub
sitting room

Beulah Land Farm is situated in the beautiful valley of the Assiniboine, in the center of Manitoba. All meals are home-grown and home-cooked.

WINNIPEG

Chestnut House
209 Chestnut St., K36 1R8
204-772-9788
John & Louise Clark
All year

$ B&B
4 rooms
C-yes

Full breakfast
Sitting room

Restored home in historic location, furnished with antiques. Close to downtown facilities, restaurants, antique shops. Full breakfast complemented by homemade baking.

More Inns...

Ernie & Tina Dyck   Box 1001, Boissevain R0K 0E0   204-534-2563
Casa Maley   1605 Victoria Ave., Brandon R7A 1C1   204-728-0812
Nancy & Geoff Tidmarch   330 Waverly St., Winnipeg R3M 3L3   204-284-3689

New Brunswick

ALBERT

Florentine Manor
R.R.2., E0A 1A0
506-882-2271
Mary & Cyril Tingley
All year

$ B&B
7 rooms, 1 pb
C-yes

Full breakfast
Lunch & dinner (request)
Two sitting rooms

Quiet, comfortable 1860's home furnished in genuine antiques. Ideal for outdoor enthusiasts—birdwatchers, bicyclists, hikers, fishermen, golfers, sightseers & photographers.

CENTREVILLE

Reid's Farm Tourist Home
RR 1, E0J 1H0
506-276-4787
Ken/Shirley Reid
All year

$ B&B/MAP
4 rooms, 2 pb
C-yes/S-no/P-no/H-ltd

Full breakfast
Lunch, tea, dinner
Sitting room
bicycles

Enjoy a rural atmosphere and old-fashioned hospitality down on the farm. We have a lake stocked with trout. Also log cabin in the woods with 5 miles of x-c trails.

GRAND MANAN ISLAND

Shorecrest Lodge
North Head, E0G 2M0
506-662-3216
Jill Malins, Frank Longstaff
Mid-May—mid-October

$ B&B
15 rooms, 3 pb
Visa, MC •
C-yes/S-yes
some French

Continental plus
Lunch, seafood dinner
Afternoon tea
Library
tennis courts nearby

Excellent bird watching, whale watching and scenic hiking trails. Owners formerly organized tours for the Canadian equivalent of the National Audubon Society.

PLASTER ROCK

Northern Wilderness Lodge
Box 571, E0J 1W0
Highway #108
506-356-8327
William Linton
All year

$ EP
14 rooms, 14 pb
Visa, MC, AmEx •
C-yes/S-yes/P-no/H-yes
English

Full breakfast $
Restaurant, bar service
Tea, snacks
sitting room
game room

Quiet, uniquely maritime—pleasant valley view—classy but country. Stroll around and through trails and forests. See country beauty for yourself.

RIVERSIDE

Cailswick Babbling Brook
Albert Co., E0A 2R0
506-882-2079
Hazen & Eunice Cail
All year

$ B&B
5 rooms, 2 pb
C-yes/S-no/P-no/H-no
French

Country breakfast
Evening snack
Sitting room
TV

Country living. Quiet, serene and restful. Home-cooked meals. Century-old Victorian overlooking Shepardy Bay, running brooks, lovely grounds. Near Fundy National Park.

ROTHESAY

Shadow Lawn Country Inn	$ EP	Full breakfast $
P.O. Box 41, E0G 2W0	8 rooms, 5 pb	Dinner by reservation
3180 Rothesay Rd.	C-yes/S-yes/P-yes/H-no	Bar service
506-847-7539	French	Sitting room, piano
Patrick & Margaret Gallagher		tennis courts
All year		

Shadow Lawn in the village of Rothesay—next to golf, tennis, sailing. Gourmet dining, with silver service.

SACKVILLE

Marshlands Inn	$ EP	Full breakfast ($)
Box 1440, E0A 3C0	25 rooms, 15 pb	Luncheon, dinner, bar
73 Bridge St.	Visa, MC, AmEx •	Sitting room
506-536-0170	C-yes/S-yes/P-ltd/H-yes	piano
John/Mary Blakley	French	
February—December		

Elegant Victorian house surrounded by trees and gardens. Adjacent Hanson House built 1890's. All furnished with antiques. Museum on grounds.

SAINT ANDREWS

Pansy Patch	$$ B&B	Full breakfast
P.O. Box 349, E0G 2X0	4 rooms	Picnic baskets w/notice
59 Carleton St.	Visa, MC, AmEx •	Sitting room, aftn. tea
506-529-3834/203-354-4181	C-yes/S-yes/P-no/H-no	snacks, library
Kathleen & Michael Lazare	English, French	tennis courts, pool
May 15—October 1		

Norman turreted home housing antique/book shop & B&B. Antique furnished bedrooms. Gourmet breakfast in garden over Passamaquoddy Bay. Private bath in June & Sept.

More Inns...

Ingle-Neuk Lodge B&B   RR 3 Box 1180, Bathurst E2A 4G8   506-546-5758
Poplars—Les Peupliers   RR1 Site 11 Box 16, Beresford E0B 1H0   506-546-5271
Compass Rose   North Head, Grand Manan E0G 2M0   506-662-8570
Cross Tree Guest House   Seal Cove, Grand Manan E0G 3B0   506-662-8263
Ferry Wharf Inn   North Head, Grand Manan E0G 2M0   506-662-8588
Grand Harbour Inn   P.O. Box 73 Grand Harbour, Grand Manan E0G 1X0   506-662-8681
Manan Island Inn & Spa   P.O. Box 15, Grand Manan E0G 2M0   506-662-8624
Eveleigh Hotel   Evandale, RR1, Hampstead E0G 1Y0   506-425-9993
Woodsview II B&B   RR 5, Hartland E0J 1N0   506-375-4637
Dutch Treat Farm   RR 1, Hopewell Cape E0A 1Y0   506-882-2552
Mactaquac B&B   Mactaquac RR1, Mactaquac E0H 1N0   506-363-3630
Governor's Mansion   Main St., Nelson E0C 1T0   506-622-3036
Different Drummer   Box 188, Sackville E0A 3C0   506-536-1291
Shiretown Inn   Town Square, St. Andrews E0G 2X0   506-529-8877
Puff'Inn   P.O. Box 135, St. Andrews E0G 2X0   506-529-4191
A Touch of Country B&B   61 Pleasant St., St. Stephen E3L 1A6   506-466-5056
Andersons Holiday Farm   Sussex RR 2, Sussex E0E 1P0   506-433-3786
Chez Prime B&B   RR3, Site 32, Losier Sttl, Tracadie E0C 2B0   506-395-6884

Nova Scotia

ANNAPOLIS ROYAL

Garrison House Inn
Box 108, B0S 1A0
350 St. George St.
902-532-5750
Patrick & Anna Redgrave
May 15—November 1

$$ EP
7 rooms, 5 pb
Visa, MC
C-ltd/S-ltd/P-no/H-no
French

Full breakfast $
Intimate 16 seat pub
Licensed dining room
Picnic lunches
sitting room, bicycles

Restored 1854 Heritage House—early Canadian antiques, hooked rugs, quilts & folk art treasures. Dining room specializes in local seafood & produce.

GUYSBOROUGH COUNTY

Liscombe Lodge
Liscomb Mills, B0J 2A0
902-779-2307
David M. Evans
June—October

$$ EP
Visa, MC, AmEx, Enr. •
C-yes/S-yes/P-ltd/H-yes

Restaurant, bar service
Afternoon tea, snacks
Sitting room, tennis
hiking, boat rentals
fishing equipment

A riverside resort, a get-away-from-it-all outdoor retreat for the entire family. Stay in chalets, cottages or the new lodge which overlooks our Marina.

HALIFAX

Apple Basket B&B
1756 Robie St., B3H 3E9
902-429-3019
Ms. Michal Crowe
All year

$ B&B
3 rooms
C-no/S-no/P-no/H-no

Continental plus

Turn-of-the-century Victorian furnished with antiques and art collection. Lovely homemade breakfast. Honeymoon special.

Queen Street Inn
1266 Queen St., B3J 2H4
902-422-9828
Alfred J. Saulnior
All year

$ EP
7 rooms, 1 pb
C-no/S-no/P-no/H-no

Old Halifax stone house built for a Nova Scotian Supreme Court Justice in 1870. Antique furnishings, in downtown Halifax.

HEBRON

Manor Inn
P.O.B. 56, Rt. 1, B0W 1X0
902-742-2487
Bev & Terry Grandy
May—December

$$ EP
Visa, MC, AmEx •
C-yes/S-yes/P-ltd/H-no
French

Full breakfast $
Lunch, dinner, bar
Entertainment
tennis courts, pool
putting green, croquet

Nine acres of landscaped grounds, formal rose garden, 3,000 feet of lakefront. Magnificent old mansion and 24-unit motel. Boating, swimming, lawn games.

PUGWASH

Blue Heron Inn
P.O. Box 405, B0K 1L0
Route 6, Durham St.
902-243-2900/902-243-2516
B. Bond & J. Caraberis
June 1—September 7

$ B&B
5 rooms, 2 pb
Visa
C-yes/S-yes/P-no/H-no

Continental breakfast
Lounge, color TV
Sitting room, piano
tennis nearby

A renovated home in the Village of Pugwash furnished with many antiques. Close to beaches, golf course and craft shops.

WOLFVILLE

Victoria's Historic Inn
Box 819, 416 Main St, B0P 1X0
902-542-5744
Ron & Doreen Cook
May—December 31

$$ B&B
15 rooms, 11 pb
MC, AmEx ●
C-yes/S-yes/P-ltd/H-yes

Full breakfast
Lunch, dinner, bar
Sitting room

Victorian inn in beautiful Nova Scotia. Interesting fireplaces in many rooms, antiques, soft music, Acadians' "Cajun cuisine". Traditional dining room.

More Inns. . .

Amherst Shore Country Inn   RR #2, Amherst B4H 3X9   902-667-4800
Bread and Roses   P.O. Box 177, Annapolis Royal B0S 1A0   902-532-5727
Cheshire Cat   Box 362, Annapolis Royal B0S 1A0   902-532-2100
Milford House   South Milford, RR #4, Annapolis Royal B0S 1A0   902-532-2617
Northhills Manor   Box 418, Granville Ferry, Annapolis Royal B0S 1A0   902-532-5555
Poplars B&B   124 Victoria St, Box 277, Annapolis Royal B0S 1A0   902-532-7936
Old Manse Inn   5 Tigo Park, Antigonish B2G 1L7   902-863-5696
Le Cape Pottery House   Queen St. P.O. Box 549, Baddeck B0E 1B0   902-295-3367
Lovett Lodge Inn   P.O. Box 119, Bear River B0S 1B0   902-467-3917
1850 House   Box 22, Main St., Canning, Kings County B0P 1H0   902-582-3052
Heart of Hart's T. H.   N.E. Margaree, Cape Breton B0E 2H0   902-248-2765
Kilmuir Place   NE Margaree, Cape Breton B0E 2H0   902-248-2877
Riverside Inn   Margaree Hrb., Cape Breton B0E 2B0   902-235-2002
McNeill Manor B&B   P.O. Box 565, Chester B0J 1J0   902-275-4638
Cobequid Hills Country Inn   Collingwood B0M 1E0   902-686-3381
Martin House   62 Pleasant St., Dartmouth B2Y 3P5   902-469-1896
Bayberry House   Box 114, Troop Ln., Granville Ferry B0S 1K0   902-532-2272
Shining Tides   RR #2, Granville Ferry B0S 1K0   902-532-2770
Seabright B&B   Seabright, Halifax County B0J 3J0   902-823-2987
Greta Cross B&B   81 Peperell St., Louisbourg B0A 1M0   902-733-2833
Boscawen Inn   P.O. Box 1343, Lunenburg B0J 2C0   902-634-3325
Chillingsworth Guest House   P.O. Box 1391, Lunenburg B0J 2C0   902-634-3701
Cape Breton Island Farm   RR 2, Mabou B0E 1X0   902-945-2077
Camelot   Box 31, Rt. 7, Musquodoboit Harbour B0J 2L0   902-889-2198
Annfield Tourist Manor   RR 3, Bras D'or, No. Sydney B0C 1B0   902-736-8770
L'Auberge   80 Front St., Box 99, Pictou B0K 1H0   902-485-6900
Westway Inn   Plympton B0W 2R0   902-837-4097
Gramma's House   RR3, Shelburne B0T 1W0   902-637-2058
Harborview Inn   P.O. Box 35, Smith's Cove, Digby Co. B0S 1S0   902-245-5686
Seabright B&B   P.O. Box 131, Tantallon B0J 3J0   902-823-2987
Lansdowne Lodge   Upper Stewiacke B0N 2P0   902-671-2749
Senator Guest House   Rt. 6, Sunrise Trail, Wallace B0K 1Y0   902-257-2417
Gilbert's Cove Farm   RR 3, Weymouth B0W 3T0   902-837-4505
Clockmaker's Inn B&B   1399 King St., Windsor   902-798-5265
Blomidon Inn   P.O. Box 839, Wolfville B0P 1X0   902-542-9326

Ontario

BRAESIDE

Glenroy Farm
RR 1, K0A 1G0
613-432-6248
Noreen & Steve McGregor
All year

$ B&B
3 rooms, 1 pb
C-yes/S-yes/P-no/H-no

Full breakfast
Dinner $5.00
Sitting room, piano
bicycles

Century-old stone farmhouse on the Ottawa River, 50 miles to Canada's Capitol. Reservations 8 am or 6 pm. Rafting, full breakfast.

BURGESSVILLE

McMillen's B&B
P.O. Box 71, N0J 1C0
41 Church St. E.
519-424-9834
All year

$$ B&B
2 rooms, 1 pb

Full breakfast
Afternoon tea (by req.)
Air-conditioned home
indoor swimming pool

McMillen's B&B is situated in a quiet village setting, close to a restaurant. Spacious bedroom. Only 10 minutes from 401. Short drive to Stratford Festival.

COBOURG

**Northumberland Heights
Country Inn**
RR 5, K9A 4J8
416-372-7500/416-372-3712
Mike & Veronica Thiele
All year

$$ EP
14 rooms, 14 pb
Visa, MC, AmEx •
C-yes/S-yes/P-no/H-yes
German, French, Dutch

Full breakfast $
Lunch, dinner, bar
Hot tub, sauna
swimming pool
sitting room, piano

Situated on 100 acres of rolling countryside. Relaxing patio areas, miniature golf, outdoor checkers, trout pond, X-c skiing, skating. Two night "plan" available.

DOWNSVIEW

Schweizer Lodge
RR 2, J0E 2K0
514-538-2129
Pauline Canzani

$ MAP

Breakfast
Dinner

Simple lodging; two persons per room; beautiful 3 bedroom house available. Quiet mountain farm setting. Meals are just great—vegetarian food on request.

GORE'S LANDING

Victoria Inn
County Rd. 18, K0K 2E0
416-342-3261
Mid-May—mid-October

$$ EP
9 rooms, 9 pb
Visa, MC, AmEx
C-ltd/S-yes/P-no/H-yes

Full breakfast $
Lunch, dinner, bar
Sitting room, piano
boat rental
swimming pool

Restful waterfront estate, stained glass windows, fireplaces highlight quaint rooms. Veranda dining room with panoramic view of Rice Lake. Boat dockage.

Kiely House Heritage Inn, Niagra-On-The-Lake, ON

MCKELLER

Inn & Tennis Club @ Manitou
P0G 1C0
416-967-3466/705-389-2171
Ben & Sheila Wise
May—October

$$$ AP
Visa, Mc, AmEx, checks •
C-yes/S-ltd
French

Full breakfast
Lunch & French dinner
Stocked library, saunas
lake, hot tubs, pool
13 tennis courts

Five-star lakeside sophisticated relais and chateaux resort. Thirteen tennis courts, luxurious suites featuring skylit sumptuous washrooms with whirlpool baths and sauna.

NEW HAMBURG

Waterlot Inn
17 Huron St., N0B 2G0
519-662-2020
Gordon Elkeer
All year

$$ B&B
3 rooms, 1 pb
Visa, MC, AmEx
C-no/S-no/P-no/H-no

Continental breakfast
Lunch, dinner, bar
Gourmet shop

Just the place for a romantic gourmet. Quiet riverside escape. One of Ontario's finest dining establishments.

OTTAWA

Albert House
478 Albert St., K1R 5B5
613-236-4479/800-267-1982
John & Cathy Delroy
All year

$$ B&B
17 rooms, 17 pb
Visa, MC, AmEx
C-yes/S-yes/P-no/H-no
French, Italian

Full breakfast
Sitting room
color cable TV in rooms
telephones

Fine restored Victorian residence designed by Thomas Seaton Scott in post-Confederate period. Complimentary breakfast, parking.

Australis Guest House
35 Marlborough Ave., K1N 8E6
613-235-8461
Carol & Brian Waters
All year

$ B&B
3 rooms, 1 pb
C-yes/S-yes/P-no/H-no

Full breakfast
Complimentary tea
Sitting room, piano
bicycles
off-street parking

An older renovated antique-filled downtown home close to all attractions in an area of embassies, parks and the river. Family suite available.

Beatrice Lyon Guest House
479 Slater St., K1R 5C2
613-236-3904
Phyllis Beatrice Lyon
All year

$ B&B
3 rooms
C-yes/S-yes/P-yes/H-no
French

Full breakfast
Afternoon tea
Living room

A 100-year-old old-fashioned family home in downtown Ottawa. 5 minutes walk to Parliament buildings, shopping, National Library, art gallery and Arts Center.

Blue Spruces
187 Glebe Ave., K1S 2C6
613-236-8521
Patricia & John Hunter
All year

$ B&B
3 rooms, 1 pb
C-6+/S-ltd/P-no/H-no
French

Full breakfast
Afternoon tea
Sitting room

Elegant Edwardian home with antiques in downtown Ottawa. Home-cooked breakfasts. We enjoy talking with guests & helping them find memorable parts of Ottawa to explore.

Cartier House Inn
46 Cartier St., K2P 1J3
613-236-INNS
Sheena Ferguson
All year

$$$ B&B
11 rooms, 11 pb
Visa, MC, AmEx ●
C-ltd/S-ltd/P-no/H-no
English, Spanish, French

Full breakfast
Afternoon tea/snacks
Jacuzzis in suites
morning paper, evening
chocolates

A "grand luxe" European inn which has been offering tranquility and an attentive staff since the turn of the century. Near the Parliament, shops and restaurants.

Doral Inn Hotel
486 Albert St., K1R 5B5
613-230-8055
Frank Baker
All year

$ EP
22 rooms, 22 pb
Visa, MC, AmEx ●
C-yes/S-yes/P-no/H-yes
French

Full breakfast
Continental restaurant
Indoor pool/spa access
sitting room, A/C
parking, TV, phones

Restored 1879 Victorian heritage home furnished in antiques, fireplaces. Centrally located in downtown; walk to tourist attractions. 4-star inn. A warm welcome awaits you.

Gasthaus Switzerland
89 Daly Ave., K1N 6E6
613-237-0335
Josef/Sabine Sauter
All year

$ B&B
17 rooms, 7 pb
Visa, MC
C-yes/S-yes/P-no/H-no
German, Serb., French

Swiss country breakfast
Afternoon tea
TV room
sitting room
barbecue, garden

Warm Swiss atmosphere in Canada's beautiful capital; clean, cozy rooms; full Swiss-continental breakfast; close to tourist attractions; free parking. Warm, clean & cheery!

Gwen's Guest Home
2071 Riverside Dr., K1H 7X2
613-737-4129
Gwen Goulding
All year

$ B&B
3 rooms
Visa, MC, AmEx, Enroute@
C-yes/S-yes/P-no/H-no

Full breakfast
Lunch, dinner
Afternoon tea, snacks
TV room, porches, picnic
garden, river, bike path

Charming 89-year-old home, furnished with antique Canadiana & handcrafts. 10 minutes from downtown. Public transportation at door.

Rideau View Inn
177 Frank St., K2P.O.X4
613-236-9309
George Hartsgrove
All year

$$ B&B
7 rooms
Visa, MC, AmEx
C-ltd/S-ltd/P-no/H-no
English, French

Full breakfast
Sitting room
bicycles
tennis nearby

Large 1907 Edwardian home with very well-appointed guest rooms. Walking distance to Parliament Hill, Rideau Canal, fine restaurants, shopping and public transport.

Westminster Guest House
446 Westminster Ave., K2A 2T8
613-729-2707
E. Deavy, K. Mikoski
All year

$ B&B
3 rooms, 1 pb
C-ltd/S-ltd/P-ltd/H-no
French

Full breakfast
Dinner by reservation
Evening refreshments
Sitting room, piano
fireplace

A turn-of-the-century home in a peaceful setting just a short drive from Parliament Hill. Close to bicycle and walking trails along Ottawa River.

PORT STANLEY ─────────────────────────

Kettle Creek Inn
Main St., N0L 2A0
519-782-3388
Gary & Jean Vedova
All year

$$ B&B
10 rooms
AmEx, Visa, MC, EnR. •
C-yes/S-yes/P-no/H-yes

Continental breakfast
Lunch, dinner, snacks
Tea, bar service
Sitting room, library
sauna, entertainment

Historic 1849 inn nestled in a quaint fishing village. Award-winning dining—indoor or outdoor in our patio and gazebo. Lovely gardens. The perfect escape.

ROCKPORT ─────────────────────────

Houseboat Amaryllis
B&B Inn
General Delivery, K0E 1V0
613-659-3513
Peter Bergen, Janet Rodier
June 1—October 15

$$ B&B
3 rooms, 3 pb
Visa, AmEx •
C-yes/S-no/P-no/H-no
Spanish, French

Full breakfast
Dinner
Sitting room
river, picnic tours in
boat rider available

Inn is a double-deck houseboat on its own 7.5-acre island. Enjoy fishing and abundant wildlife. Private baths. Gourmet meals.

SAINT JACOBS ─────────────────────────

Jakobstettel Guest House
16 Isabella St., N0B 2N0
P.O. Box 28
519-664-2208
Ella Brubacher
All year

$$$ B&B
12 rooms, 12 pb
Visa, MC, AmEx
C-yes/S-ltd/P-no/H-no
Pennsylvania German

Continental plus
Tea, coffee, snacks
Swimming pool, trail
tennis courts, bicycles
sitting room, library

Luxurious privacy set amidst 5 acres w/trees. Each room decorated with its own charm & Victorian features. Local artisan shops withing walking distance.

TORONTO

Ashleigh Heritage Home
42 Delaware Ave., M6H 2S7
416-535-4000
Gwen Lee
All year

$ B&B
4 rooms
Visa •
C-yes/S-ltd/P-no/H-no

Continental plus
Sitting room, piano
bicycles, library
parking

Restored 1910 home with interesting architectural details and a large garden. Just minutes from the University, the museum and government offices.

Burken Guest House
322 Palmerston Blvd., M6G 2N6
416-920-7842
K. Bosher/B. Friedrichkeit
All year

$ B&B
8 rooms
Visa, MC •
C-yes/S-yes/P-no/H-no
German, French

Continental plus
Deck, garden
parking

Very attractive home in charming downtown residential area. Period furniture, close to Eaton Centre. Weekly rates available.

More Inns. . .

Horseshoe Inn   RR 2, Alton L0N 1A0   519-927-5779
Galetta Guest House   RR #1, Arnprior K7S 3G7   613-623-7020
Little Inn of Bayfield   P.O. Box 100, Bayfield N0M 1G0   519-565-2611
Landfall Farm   RR1, Blackstock L0B 1B0   416-986-5588
Holiday House Inn   P.O. Box 1139, Bracebridge P0B 1C0   705-645-2245
Country Guest Home   RR 2, Bradford L3Z 2A5   416-775-3576
Caledon Inn   Caledon East L0N 1E0   416-584-2891
Ottawa Valley B&B   96 Lake Ave. W., Carleton Place K7C 1L8   613-257-7720
Magerson Guest Home   RR2, Carp K0A 1L0   613-839-2890
Chestnut Inn   9 Queen St., Cookstown L0L 1L0   705-458-9751
Sir Sam's Inn   Eagle Lake Post Office, Eagle Lake K0M 1M0   705-754-2188
Lucky Lancione's   635 Metler Rd. RR3, Fenwick L0S 1C0   416-892-8104
Breadelbane Inn   487 St. Andrew St. W., Fergus N1M 1P2   519-843-4770
Bushland Meadows   Box 224, Flesherton N0C 1E0   519-924-2675
Glencairn Manor   P.O. Box 22, Glencairn L0M 1K0   705-424-6045
Cedarlane Farm B&B   R.R. 2, Iroquois K0E 1K0   613-652-4267
Prince George Hotel   200 Ontario St., Kingston K7L 2Y9   613-549-5440
Ivy Lea Inn   1000 Isl. Pkwy., Lansdowne K0E 1L0   613-659-2329
Rose B&B   526 Dufferin Ave., London N6B 2A2   519-433-9978
Bea's B&B House   Box 133, Maynooth K0L 2S0   613-338-2239
Minden House   P.O. Box 789, Minden K0M 2K0   705-286-3263
Sterling Lodge   Newboro K0G 1P0   613-272-2435
Kiely House Heritage Inn   P.O. Box 1642, Niagara-On-The-Lake L0S 1J0   416-468-4588
Angel Inn   224 Regent St., Niagara-on-the-lake L0S 1J0   416-468-3411
Kiely House Heritage Inn   209 Queen St. Box 1642, Niagara-on-the-lake L2G 6R5   416-468-4588
Paines' B&B   Carling Bay Rd., RR1, Nobel P0G 1G0   705-342-9266
Union Hotel   Box 38, RR 1, Normandale N0E 1W0   519-426-5568
Willi-Joy Farm   RR #3, Norwich N0J 1P0   519-424-2113
Al Leclerc's Residence   253-McLeod St., Ottawa K2P 1A1   613-234-7577
Constance House B&B   62 Sweetland Ave., Ottawa K1N 7T6   613-235-8888
Flora House   282 Flora St., Ottawa K1R 5S3   613-230-2152
Haydon House   18 Queen Elizabeth Drwy., Ottawa K2P 1C6   613-230-2697
O'Conner House Downtown   172 O'Conner St., Ottawa K2P 1T5   613-236-4221
Rideau View Inn   177 Frank St, Ottawa K2P.O.X4   613-236-9309
Moses Sunset Farms B&B   RR6, Owen Sound N4K 5N8   519-371-4559

Rebecca's B&B   P.O. Box 1028, Petrolia N0N 1R0   519-882-0118
Sherwood Inn   P.O. Box 400, Port Carling P0B 1J0   705-765-3131
Good Old British B&B   4 Ransford St., Port Franks N0M 2L0   519-243-3694
Arrowwood Lodge   P.O. Box 125, Port Severn L0K 1S0   705-538-2354
Burnside Guest Home   139 William St., Stratford N5A 4X9   519-271-7076
Jester Arms Inn   P.O. Box 1007, Stratford N5A 6W4   519-271-1121
Shrewsbury Manor   30 Shrewsbury St., Stratford N5A 2V5   519-271-8520
Mrs. Mitchell's   Violet Hill L0N 1S0   819-925-3672
Windermere House   Windermere P0B 1P0   705-769-3611
Old Bridge Inn   Young's Point K0L 3G0   705-652-8507

Prince Edward Island

CHARLOTTETOWN

Barachois Inn
P.O. Box 1022, C1A 7M4
Church Rd., Rt. 243
902-963-2194
Judy & Gary MacDonald
May 1—October 31

$ EP
6 rooms, 1 pb
C-yes/S-no/P-no/H-no
English, French

Full breakfast $
Sitting room
pump organ

Victorian house offers lovely views of bay, river and countryside. Antique furnishings and modern comforts. Walk to seashore.

Stanhope by the Sea
P.O. Box 2109, C1A 7N7
Stanhope
902-672-2047/902-892-6008
Dr. A. & Dr. C. Tadros
June—September 1

$$ EP
Visa, MC •
C-yes/S-yes/P-yes/H-no
French

Full breakfast
Lunch, dinner, bar
Sitting room, piano
entertainment, tennis
bikes, golf, surfing

Furnished with period antiques, resort setting, National Park beaches, sand dunes, windsurfing, bicycle packages and all-you-can-eat lobster smorgasbord daily.

KENSINGTON

Sherwood Acres Guest Home
RR 1, C0B 1M0
902-836-5430
Erma & James Hickey
All year

$ B&B
6 rooms, 1 pb
C-yes/S-yes/P-yes/H-yes

Continental plus
Sitting room
piano

Near lovely sandy beaches, clam digging, country walks. Food is all homemade, including the bread and butter. Also private house available by the week.

MURRAY RIVER

Bayberry Cliff Inn B&B Ltd.
RR 4, Little Sands, C0A 1W0
902-962-3395
Nancy & Don Perkins
May 15—September 30

$ B&B
7 rooms
Visa, MC
C-yes
Spanish

Full breakfast
Sitting room, library
craft shop, stairs down
40 ft cliff to shore

Two remodeled post & beam barns 50 feet from edge of cliff. Furnishings: antiques, marine paintings. 8 minutes to W.I.'s ferry. Five levels.

STANHOPE —————————————————————————————————

Stanhope by the Sea	$$ EP	Restaurant, bar service
P.O. Box 2109	35 rooms, 35 pb	Lunch, dinner
Route 25	Visa, MC •	Sitting room, library
902-672-2047	C-yes/S-yes/P-ltd/H-yes	bicycles
June 1—September 30	French	tennis courts

Oldest summer resort on Prince Edward Island on the beach; golf next door; windsurfer paradise. Gourmet dining; a real treat for the entire family.

SUMMERSIDE —————————————————————————————————

Silver Fox Inn	$ B&B	Continental breakfast
61 Granville St., C1N 2Z3	6 rooms, 6 pb	Sitting room
902-436-4033	Visa, MC, AmEx •	piano
Julie Simmons	C-no/S-yes/P-no/H-no	
All year		

Restored 1892 house with antique furnishings. Sun room, sitting room with fireplace, and balcony for guests. Breakfast with homemade muffins, jams, farm eggs.

More Inns...

Shore Farm B&B   Borden RR1, Augustine Cove C0B 1X0   902-855-2871
Linden Lodge   RR 3, Belfast C0A 1A0   902-659-2716
Churchill Farm T.H.   RR3, Bonshaw C0A 1C0   902-675-2481
Shaw's Hotel & Cottages   Brackley Beach C0A 2H0   902-672-2022
Windsong Farm B&B   Winsloe RR #1, Brackley Beach C0A 2H0   902-672-2874
Allix's B&B   11 Johnson Av., Charlottetown C1A 3H7   902-892-2643
Just Folks B&B   RR 5, Charlottetown C1A 7J8   902-569-2089
Rosevale Farm B&B   Marshfield, RR 3, Charlottetown C1A 7J7   902-894-7821
Obanlea Farm Tourist Home   RR 4 No. River P.O., Cornwall C0A 1H0   902-566-3067
Chez-Nous B&B   Ferry Rd., RR 4, Corwan C0A 1H0   902-566-2779
Fralor Farm Tourist Home   RR 1, Kensington, Darnley C0B 1M0   902-836-5300
Beach Pt. View Country Inn   RR 5, Kensington C0B 1M0   902-836-5260
Blakeney's B&B   15 MacLean Ave, Box 17, Kensington C0B 1M0   902-836-3254
Murphy's Sea View B&B   Rte.20, Kensington C0B 1M0   902-836-5456
Woodington's Country Inn   Sea View, RR 2, Kensington C0B 1M0   902-836-5518
Dalvay by the Sea Hotel   P.O. Box 8, Little York C0A 1P0   902-672-2048
Waugh's Farm B&B   Lower Bedeque C0B 1C0   902-887-2320
Rosevale Farm B&B   Charlottetown RR3, Marshfield C1A 7J7   902-894-7821
Carr's Corner Farm   Rt. 12, Miscouche C0B 1T0   902-436-6287
Brydon's B&B   Heatherdale RR 1, Montague C0A 1R0   902-838-4747
Harbourview B&B   RR 1, Murray Harbour C0A 1V0   902-962-2565
Andrew Lodge-Cottages   New Glasgow G0A 1N0   902-964-2508
Laine Acres B&B   Cornwall RR2, Nine Mile Creek C0A 1H0   902-675-2402
Joyce's Tourist Home   North Rustico C0A 1X0   902-963-2257
Smallman's B&B   Knutsford, RR 1, O'Leary C0B 1V0   902-859-3469
Partridge's B&B   RR 2, Montague, Panmure Island C0A 1R0   902-838-4687
MacCallum's B&B   Rt. 2, St. Peters Bay C0A 2A0   902-961-2957
Creekside Farm B&B   Stanley Bridge C0A 1E0   902-886-2713
Gulf Breeze   Stanley Bridge C0A 1E0   902-886-2678
Faye & Eric's B&B   380 Mac Ewen Rd., Summerside C1N 4X8   902-436-6847
Harbour Lights T. H.   RR #2, Tignish C0B 2B0   902-882-2479
Doctor's Inn B&B   Tyne Valley C0B 2C0   902-831-2164
West Island Inn   Box 24, Tyne Valley C0B 2C0   902-831-2495

MacLeod's Farm B&B   UIGG, Vernon P.O., Vernon C0A 2E0   902-651-2303
Enman's Farm B&B   P.O. RR2 Vernon Bridge, Vernon Bridge C0A 2E0   902-651-2427
Lea's B&B   Vernon River C0A 2E0   902-651-2501
Victoria Village Inn   Victoria-by-the-Sea C0A 2G0   902-658-2288
Amber Lights B&B   P.O. Box 14, Rte.26, York C0A 1P0   902-894-5868

Quebec

HUBERDEAU

Otter Lake Haus
C.S. 29, CH Trudel, J0T 1G0
819-687-2767
F. Thiel
except November

$ MAP
22 rooms, 9 pb
Credit cards accepted •
C-yes/S-yes/P·ltd/H-ltd
French, German

Full breakfast
Lunch, dinner, bar
Tennis courts, bicycles
sitting room, piano
lake swimming

65 km cross-country ski trails, lake & boats, cozy family atmosphere, home-cooked meals. AP and MAP also available.

KAMOURASKA

Gite du Passant B&B
81 Ave. Morel, G0L 1M0
418-492-2921
Mariette Le Blanc
May 1—November 1

$ B&B
3 rooms, 3 pb
C-ltd/S-no/P-no/H-no
French

Full breakfast
Sitting room
piano

Venez voir notre beau village situe sur le bord du fleuve, dans une ancienne maison renove. Magnifique couche de soleil.

KNOWLTON

Auberge Laketree
RR 2, Stagecoach Rd., J0E 1V0
514-243-6604
Ursula Seebohm
ex. April & November

$ B&B
8 rooms, 3 pb
C-yes/S-ltd/P-no/H-yes
English, French, German

Full breakfast
Bicycles
sitting room
piano

Food organic, varied and plenty. The inn is artistic and spacious, fits 20. The view is unique over mountains and lake. Gemutlichkeit, ski trails—here is your break!

MONT TREMBLANT

Chateau Beauvallon, Inc.
Montee Ryan, Box 138, J0T 1Z0
819-425-7275
Judy & Alex Riddell
ex. October 15—November 25

$$ MAP
14 rooms, 7 pb
•
C-yes/S-yes/P-ltd/H-ltd
French

Full breakfast
Dinner, bar
Sitting room, piano
bicycles
lake swimming

Country inn with home cooking, on a clear quiet mountain lake. Cycling, golf, tennis, windsurfing, all available within two-mile proximity.

MONTREAL

Armor Inn
151 Sherbrooke E., H2X 1C7
514-285-0894
Annick Morvan
All year

$ EP
14 rooms, 7 pb
•
C-yes/S-yes/P-no/H-no
French

Comp. coffee

Once a fine Victorian townhouse in downtown Montreal. Fine woodwork in foyer and some guest rooms.

POINTE-AU-PIC

Auberge Donohue
145 Principale,
C.P. 211, G0T 1M0
418-665-4377
Monique & Orval Aumont
All year

$$$ B&B
13 rooms, 13 pb
C-ltd/S-yes/P-no/H-no
French

Continental breakfast
Afternoon tea
Sitting room, piano
swimming pool
fireplaces

Cozy house situated right by the St. Lawrence River. Very large living room with fireplace. Every room has private bath; most rooms have view of the river.

PORTNEUF

Edale Place
Edale Pl., G0A 2Y0
418-286-3168
Mary & Tam Farnsworth
All year

$ B&B
4 rooms
C-yes/S-yes/P-no/H-no
French

Full breakfast
Afternoon tea
Sitting room
jacuzzi
15% reduction for skiers

Victorian country home. Beautiful, peaceful, quiet spot. 35-minute drive from Quebec City.

QUEBEC CITY

Au Manoir Ste-Genevieve
13 Ave. Ste-Genevieve, G1R 4A7
418-694-1666
Marguerite Coriveau
All year

$$ EP
9 rooms, 9 pb
C-yes/S-yes/P-no/H-no
French

Fresh cut flowers &
window boxes

Manor with modern facilities, furnished with antiques. Friendly and comfortable. Located behind Chateau Frontenac, on the St. Lawrence River. Walk to all points of interest.

Le Chateau De Pierre
17 Ave. Ste-Genevieve, G1R 4A8
418-694-0429
Lily Couturier
All year

$$$ EP
15 rooms, 15 pb
Visa, MC
C-yes/S-ltd/P-no/H-no
French, Spanish

Kitchenettes in 2 units
color TVs
air conditioned

Old English colonial mansion with colonial charm. Fine appointments and distinctive atmosphere. Located in Old Quebec Uppertown. Walk to Citadel, shopping, historical points.

Maison Marie-Rollet
81, rue Ste-Anne, G1R 3X4
418-694-9271
Fernand Blouin
All year

$$ EP
10 rooms, 10 pb
Visa •
C-yes/S-yes/P-no/H-no
French

Well-situated, in the center of Old Quebec facing the City Hall. Parking across the street. Quiet Victorian house.

SAINT ANNE DES MONT

Gite du Mont Albert	$ B&B/MAP	Full breakfast
Case Postale 1150, G0E 2G0	Visa, MC, AmEx, EnR. •	Restaurant, bar service
418-763-2288/800-463-0860	C-yes/S-yes/H-yes	Comp. wine, snacks
Stephanie Barriere	French	Pool, hot tubs, sauna
March 1—January 3		bicycles, fishing, ski

An inn renowned for its cuisine & its exceptional surroundings. Activities: hiking, fishing, canoeing & sailing, cycling in the mountains, nature interpretation, skiing.

SAINT ANTOINE DE TILLY

Auberge Manoir de Tilly	$$ B&B/MAP	Full breakfast
3854 Chemin de Tilly, G0S 2C0	12 rooms, 7 pb	Dinner available
418-886-2407/418-886-2595	Visa, MC, AmEx, EnRoute	Piano, swimming pool
Jocelyne & Majella Gagnon	C-yes/S-ltd/P-no/H-no	bicycles, shuffleboard
April 1—December 31	French, English	golf, tennis nearby

200-year-old manor on St. Lawrence River shores. Furnished in antiques. 15 miles from Quebec Bridge (gate of Old City). Antique stores nearby.

SUTTON

Auberge Schweizer	$ B&B	Full breakfast
357 Schweizer, J0E 2K0	11 rooms, 2 pb	Afternoon tea, snacks
514-538-2129	Visa •	Swimming pool
Pauline Canzani	C-yes/S-yes/P-no/H-no	hiking, x-c skiing
All year	French, German Swiss	farm, animals

A truly cozy hideaway with a commanding view over the entire Sutton Valley. Simple, but clean facilities and a proverbial Swiss cuisine.

More Inns. . .

La Maison Otis   23 R. St. Jean Baptiste, Baie St. Paul G0A 1B0   418-435-2255
Hostellerie Rive Gauche   1810 boul. Richelieu, Beloeil J3G 4S4   514-467-4650
Auberge La Pinsonniere   124 St. Raphael, Cap-a-l'Aigle G0T 1B0   418-665-4431
La Pinsonniere   124 St. Raphael, Cap-a-l'Aigle G0T 1B0   418-665-4431
Auberge Le Coin Du Banc   Rt. 132, Coin du Banc-Perce G0C 2L0   418-645-2907
Willow Inn   208 Main Rd., Como J0P 1A0   514-458-7006
Auberge La Martre   La Martre, Comte de Mantane G0E 2H0   418-288-5533
Gite du Passant   136 Ave. Rious Mont Joli, Cte. Matapedia G5H 1Z1   418-775-5237
Maplewood   Malenfant Rd., Dunham J0E 1M0   514-295-2519
Henry House   105 DuParc, St. Simeon, Gaspesie G0C 3A0   418-534-2115
Georgeville Country Inn   CP P.O. Box 17, Georgeville J0B 1T0   819-843-8683
Hazelbrae Farm   1650 English River Rd., Howick J0S 1G0   514-825-2390
Leduc   1128CH Riviere de Guerre, Huntington, St. Anicet J0S 1M0   514-264-6533
Chez les Dumas   1415 Chemin Royal, St. L, Ile d'Orleans G0A 3Z0   418-828-9442
Manor De L'Anse   22 Av. du Quai, Ile d'Orleans G0A 4C0   418-828-2248
Auburg du Pain Chaud,   phone has been disconected, Lac Saquay   819-278-3226
Auberge Sauvignon   Rte #327, Mont Tremblant J0T 1Z0   819-425-2658
Manoir des Erables   220 Du Manoir, Perce, Montmagny G54V 1G   418-248-0100
Antonio Costa   101 Northview, Montreal H4X 1C9   514-486-6910
Le Breton   1609 St. Hubert, Montreal East H2L 3Z1   514-524-7273
Auberge Hollandaise   Rt. 329, Morin Heights G0R 1H0   514-226-2009
Hotel la Normandie   P.O. Box 129, Perce, Gaspe Peninsula G0G 2L0   418-782-2112
France Beaulieu House   211Chemin de la Traverse, Portneuf G0A 2Y0   418-336-2724
B&B Bonjour Quebec   3765, BD Monaco, Quebec G1P 3J3   418-527-1465
Au Chateau Fleur de Lis   15 Ave. Ste. Genevieve, Quebec City G1R 4A8   418-694-1884

Auberge St-Denis 61, St-Denis, CP 1229, Saint Sauveur Des Monts J0R 1R0 514-227-4766
Auberge De La Chouette 71 Rue D'Auteuil, Quebec City G1K 5Y4 418-694-0232
Chateau de la Terrasse 6 Terrasse Dufferin, Quebec City G1R 4N5 418-694-9472
Memory Lane Farm RR #1, Quyon J0X 2V0 819-458-2479
Handfield Inn 555 Chemin du Prince, St-Marc-sur-Richelieu J0L 2E0 514-584-2226
Maison sous les Arbres 145 Chemin Royal, St. Laurent G0A 3Z0 418-828-9442
Hostellerie de 3 Tilleuls 290 rue Richelieu, St. Marc Sur Richelieu J0L 2E0 514-584-2231
Pelletier House 334 de la Seigneurie, St. Roch des Aulnaies G0R 4E0 418-354-2450
Auberge La Goeliche Inn 22 Rue du Quai, Ste. Petronille G0A 4C0 418-828-2248
Auberge Historique 736 Chemin Draper Rd. RR4, Sutton J0E 2K0 514-538-3120
Auberge Le Rucher C.P. 1059, Val David J0T 2N0 819-322-2507
Auberge du Vieux Foyer 3167 Doncaster, Val David J0T 2N0 819-322-2686
Parker's Lodge 1340 Lac Paquin, Val David J0T 2N0 819-322-2026
Au Petit Hotel 3 Ruelle des Ursulines, Vieux-Quebec G1R 3Y6 418-694-0965
Perras 1552 RR 1, Waterloo J0E 1N0 514-539-2983

Saskatchewan

BULYEA

Hillcrest Hotel	$ EP	All meals, full bar
Box 98, S0G 0L0	7 rooms	Sitting room, piano
306-725-4874	C-yes/S-yes/P-yes/H-no	entertainment
W. & A. Nosen	German	bicycles
All year		

Prairie inn and pub furnished in antiques, collectibles—10 minutes from Inland Lake. Ice fishing, hunting, boating, rodeos, country music festival.

BURSTALL

Tiger Lily Farm	$ B&B	Full breakfast
Box 135, S0N 0H0	3 rooms, 2 pb	All meals if ordered
306-679-4709	C-yes/S-yes/P-yes/H-yes	Hot tub, bicycles
Ray		sitting room
All year		library

Plenty of Canadian geese in the fall. Good meals.

TISDALE

Prairie Acres B&B	$ EP/$$ B&B/MAP/AP	Full breakfast
Box 1658, S0E 1T0	5 rooms, 2 pb	Lunch, dinner
306-873-2272	C-yes/P-ltd/H-yes	Afternoon tea, snacks
Kathleen & Clarence Reed		Library, bikes, hot tubs
All year		hiking trails, massage

Beautiful hillside setting, tall spruce trees, wildlife, deer, Canada geese, beaver. Breakfast in beautiful flower garden. Relax in the hot tub.

More Inns...

Moldenhauer's Farm   Box 214, Allan S0K 0C0   306-257-3578
Ellis Farm   Box 84, Balcarres S0G 0C0   306-334-2238
Vereshagin's Country Place   Box 89, Blaine Lake S0J 0J0   306-497-2782
Sargent's Holiday Farm   Box 204, Borden S0K 0N0   306-997-2230
Magee's Farm   Box 654, Gull Lake S0N 1A0
Hearn's Manor House   Box 1177, Indian Head S0G 2K0   306-695-3837
Sugden Simmental Farm B&B   Box 2, Peebles S0G 3V0   306-697-3169
B&J's Bed & Breakfast   2066 Ottawa St., Regina S4P 1P8   306-522-4575
Turgeon Int' B&B   2310 McIntyre St., Regina S4P 2S2   306-522-4200
Dee Bar One   Box 51, Truax S0H 4A0   306-868-4614
Eastons' Farm   Box 58, Wawota S0G 5A0   306-739-2910
Pleasant Vista Angus Farm   Box 194, Wawota S0G 5A0   306-739-2915

Reservation Service Organizations

These are businesses through which you can reserve a room in thousands of private homes. In many cases rooms in homes are available where there may not be an inn. Also, guesthouses are quite inexpensive. RSO's operate in different ways. Some represent a single city or state. Others cover the entire country. Some require a small membership fee. Others sell a list of their host homes. Many will attempt to match you with just the type of accommodations you're seeking and you may pay the RSO directly for your lodging.

Reservation Service Organizations by Region—See main RSO listings under the state headings for full description.

Northeast

B&B Ltd.
New Haven, CT

Covered Bridge B&B
Norfolk, CT

Alexander's B&B Res. Service
Salisbury, CT

B&B of Delaware
Wilmington, DE

B&B of Maine
Falmouth, ME

Traveller in Maryland, Inc.
Annapolis, MD

Amanda's B&B Reservation
Baltimore, MD

B&B Marblehead & Northshore
Beverly, MA

B&B Agency of Boston
Boston, MA

B&B Associates Bay Colony
Boston, MA

Host Homes of Boston
Boston, MA

Folkestone B&B
Boylston, MA

Greater Boston Hospitality
Brookline, MA

B&B Cambridge & Gr. Boston
Cambridge, MA

Pineapple Hospitality, Inc.
New Bedford, MA

House Guests Cape Cod & Isl.
Orleans, MA

Be Our Guest, B&B, Ltd.
Plymouth, MA

B&B/The National Network
Springfield, MA

B&B Cape Cod
West Hyannisport, MA

Berkshire Bed & Breakfast
Williamsburg, MA

B&B of New Jersey
Highland Park, NJ

B&B of Princeton
Princeton, NJ

B&B USA Ltd.
Croton-on-Hudson, NY

Hampton Bed & Breakfast
East Moriches, NY

B&B Rochester
Fairport, NY

B&B Leatherstocking
Frankfort, NY

North Country B&B Res. Serv.
Lake Placid, NY

. . . Aaah! B&B #1, Ltd.
New York, NY

Abode B&B Ltd.
New York, NY

B&B (& Books)
New York, NY

B&B Network of New York
New York, NY

New World B&B
New York, NY

Urban Ventures, Inc.
New York, NY

American Country Collection
Schenectady, NY

B&B of Greater Syracuse
Syracuse, NY

B&B of Philadelphia
Chester Springs, PA

B&B Connections
Devon, PA

B&B—The Manor
Havertown, PA

B&B of Chester County
Kennett Square, PA

Pittsburgh B&B
Pittsburgh, PA

B&B of Valley Forge
Valley Forge, PA

Guesthouses, Inc
West Chester, PA

Anna's Victorian Connection
Newport, RI

B&B of Rhode Island
Newport, RI

Guest House Assoc. of Newport
Newport, RI

Newport Reservation Service
Newport, RI

B&B League, Ltd.
Washington, DC

Bed 'n' Breakfast Ltd.
Washington, DC

Sweet Dreams & Toast
Washington, DC

Southeast

Bed & Breakfast Birmingham
Birmingham, AL

B&B Montgomery
Millbrook, AL

B&B of the Florida Keys
Marathon, FL

Central Florida B&B
Ocala, FL

B&B Atlanta
Atlanta, GA

R.S.V.P. Savannah B&B
Savannah, GA

**Savannah Historic Inns
& Guest Houses**
Savannah, GA

Quail Country B&B
Thomasville, GA

B&B of New Jersey
Highland Park, NJ
Charleston Society B&B
Charleston, SC
Historic Charleston B&B
Charleston, SC
Charleston East B&B League
Mount Pleasant, SC
Princely B&B Ltd.
Alexandria, VA
Guesthouses B&B
Charlottesville, VA
B&B of Tidewater Virginia
Norfolk, VA
Bensonhouse
Richmond, VA
Travel Tree
Williamsburg, VA

North Central

B&B/Chicago
Chicago, IL
B&B in Iowa, Ltd.
Preston, IA
B&B Kansas City
Lenexa, KS
Ohio Valley B&B, Inc.
Independence, KY
Kentucky Homes B&B, Inc.
Louisville, KY
Bluegrass B&B
Versailles, KY
B&B in Michigan
Dearborn, MI
Go Native...Hawaii
Lansing, MI
Ozark Mountain Country B&B
Branson, MO
B&B St. Louis
Saint Louis, MO
B&B of the Great Plains
Lincoln, NE
B&B of New Jersey
Highland Park, NJ
Private Lodgings, Inc.
Cleveland, OH
South Dakota B&B
Sioux Falls, SD
B&B Guest Homes
Algoma, WI
B&B of Milwaukee, Inc.
Milwaukee, WI

South Central

Arkansas & Ozarks B&B
Calico Rock, AR
**B&B Reservation Services
Tourist Accommodations**
Eureka Springs, AR
**B&B Reservation Services
Worldwide**
Baton Rouge, LA
Southern Comfort B&B
Baton Rouge, LA
New Orleans B&B
New Orleans, LA
Lincoln Ltd. B&B
Meridian, MS
**Creative Travel B&B Center
Canal Street Depot**
Natchez, MS
B&B of New Jersey
Highland Park, NJ
B&B in Memphis
Memphis, TN
B&B Host Homes of Tennessee
Nashville, TN
B&B of Fredericksburg
Fredericksburg, TX
Gasthaus Schmidt
Fredericksburg, TX

Northwest

**Accommodations Alaska Style
Stay with a Friend**
Anchorage, AK
**Alaska Private Lodgings
Anchorage B&B**
Anchorage, AK
Fairbanks B&B
Fairbanks, AK
Alaska B&B Assoc.
Juneau, AK
Kodiak B&B
Kodiak, AK
B&B International
Albany, CA
B&B Exchange
Calistoga, CA
B&B of Idaho
Boise, ID
B&B Western Adventure
Billings, MT

B&B of New Jersey
Highland Park, NJ
Country Host Registry
Myrtle Creek, OR
Northwest B&B Travel Unltd.
Portland, OR
Pacific B&B Agency
Seattle, WA

Southwest

B&B In Arizona
Scottsdale, AZ
B&B Scottsdale
Scottsdale, AZ
Valley o' the Sun B&B
Scottsdale, AZ
Mi Casa Su Casa B&B
Tempe, AZ
Old Pueblo Homestays B&B RSO
Tucson, AZ
B&B International
Albany, CA
Eye Openers B&B Reservations
Altadena, CA
Digs West
Buena Park, CA
B&B Exchange
Calistoga, CA
B&B Homestay
Cambria, CA
**Carolyn's B&B Homes in
San Diego**
Chula Vista, CA
B&B of Southern California
Fullerton, CA
Mendocino Coast Reservations
Mendocino, CA
B&B Hospitality
Oceanside, CA
B&B Exchange of Marin
San Anselmo, CA
American Family Inn/B&B SF
San Francisco, CA
Hospitality Plus
San Juan Capistro, CA
**Megan's Friends B&B
Reservations**
San Luis Obispo, CA
California Houseguests Int'l.
Tarzana, CA

CoHost, America's B&B
Whittier, CA

B&B Colorado Ltd.
Boulder, CO

B&B Rocky Mountains & Skiers
Colorado Springs, CO

B&B Vail/Ski Areas
Vail, CO

B&B Honolulu
Honolulu, HI

B&B Pacific-Hawaii
Kailua, Oahu, HI

B&B Hawaii
Kapaa, HI

B&B Maui Style
Kihei, Maui, HI

B&B of New Jersey
Highland Park, NJ

B&B of Santa Fe
Santa Fe, NM

B&B Texas Style
Dallas, TX

Eastern Canada

First Choice B&B Agency
Vancouver, BC

London/Area B&B Association
London, ON

Niagara Region B&B Service
Niagara Falls, ON

Ottawa Area B&B
Ottawa, ON

Downtown Toronto Assoc. B&B
Toronto, ON

Toronto B&B (1987) Inc.
Toronto, ON

B&B Montreal
Montreal, PQ

B&B Network Hospitality
Montreal, PQ

Downtown B&B Network
Montreal, PQ

Western Canada

Born Free B&B of B.C. Ltd.
Burnaby, BC

Vancouver B&B Ltd.
Burnaby, BC

Old English B&B Registry
North Vancouver, BC

AB&C B&B of Vancouver
Vancouver, BC

Town & Country B&B in B.C.
Vancouver, BC

All Season B&B Agency
Victoria, BC

Garden City B&B
Victoria, BC

B&B of Manitoba
Winnipeg, MB

International

Accommodations Alaska Style Stay with a Friend
Anchorage, AK

Digs West
Buena Park, CA

Carolyn's B&B Homes in San Diego
Chula Vista, CA

California Houseguests Int'l.
Tarzana, CA

CoHost, America's B&B
Whittier, CA

B&B Rocky Mountains & Skiers
Colorado Springs, CO

Central Florida B&B
Ocala, FL

B&B in Iowa, Ltd.
Preston, IA

Ohio Valley B&B, Inc.
Independence, KY

Southern Comfort B&B
Baton Rouge, LA

New Orleans B&B
New Orleans, LA

Traveller in Maryland, Inc.
Annapolis, MD

B&B Marblehead & Northshore
Beverly, MA

Pineapple Hospitality, Inc.
New Bedford, MA

House Guests Cape Cod & Isl.
Orleans, MA

Lincoln Ltd. B&B
Meridian, MS

Natchez Pilgrimage Tours
Natchez, MS

B&B of the Great Plains
Lincoln, NE

B&B of New Jersey
Highland Park, NJ

B&B USA Ltd.
Croton-on-Hudson, NY

Urban Ventures, Inc.
New York, NY

Northwest B&B Travel Unltd.
Portland, OR

B&B of Philadelphia
Chester Springs, PA

B&B of Valley Forge
Valley Forge, PA

Guesthouses, Inc
West Chester, PA

Charleston East B&B League
Mount Pleasant, SC

B&B Host Homes of Tennessee
Nashville, TN

B&B Texas Style
Dallas, TX

Gasthaus Schmidt
Fredericksburg, TX

All Season B&B Agency
Victoria, BC

ALABAMA

Bed & Breakfast Birmingham
P.O. Box 31328
Birmingham, AL 35222

205-933-2704
$

B&B Montgomery
P.O. Box 886
Millbrook, AL 36054

205-285-5421
$
Dep. $20

Free brochure
Alabama
24 hr ans mach

More RSO's...

B&B Alabama, Inc.   P.O. Box 31328, Birmingham 35222   205-591-6406
B&B Mobile   P.O. Box 66261, Mobile 36606   205-473-2939

ALASKA

Accommodations Alaska Style
Stay with a Friend
3605 Arctic Blvd. Box 173
Anchorage, AK 99503

907-344-4006
$
$35 dep. or Cr Cd
Visa, MC

Brochure SASE
Alaska
9-9, May-October
9-12, Nov-April

Alaska Private Lodgings
Anchorage B&B
1236 W. 10th Ave.
Anchorage, AK 99501

907-258-1717
$35-80
Dep. 1 night
Ger,Fr,Sp

Free Brochure
Alaska
9am-5pm

Fairbanks B&B
P.O. Box 74573
Fairbanks, AK 99707

907-452-4967
$$
Dep. 25%
Visa, MC

Free Brochure
Alaska
all year

Alaska B&B Assoc.
P.O. Box 1321
Juneau, AK 99802

907-586-2959
$
Dep $25
Visa MC AE
German

Free Brochure
Southeast Alaska
9am-5pm

Kodiak B&B
308 Cope St.
Kodiak, AK 99615

907-486-5367
$55
Dep. $10
Sp

Brochure
Alaska
evenings/weekends

More RSO's...

Ketchikan B&B   P.O. Box 7735, Ketchikan 99801   907-225-3860

ARIZONA

B&B In Arizona
P.O. Box 8628
Scottsdale, AZ 85252

602-995-2831
$
Dep. 1 night
Visa/MC/AmEx

Free brochure
Listing $3
AZ
M-F 10am-6pm
Sat-Sun 10am-2pm

B&B Scottsdale
P.O. Box 3999
Scottsdale, AZ 85302-3999

602-776-1102
$
Dep. 25%-50%

Free brochure
AZ & Pacifc Coast
24 hours

Valley o' the Sun B&B P.O. Box 2214 Scottsdale, AZ 85252	602-941-1281 $ Dep. 1 night	Free Brochure AZ 6 days 9am-5pm
Mi Casa Su Casa B&B P.O. Box 950 Tempe, AZ 85281	602-990-0682 $ Dep. $25 Fr,Ger,Sp,It,Port	Directory $3 Arizona NM, UT 8am-8pm daily
Old Pueblo Homestays B&B RSO P.O. Box 13603 Tucson, AZ 85732	602-790-2399 $ Dep. $15	Brochure SASE Tuscon, AZ only 24 hour ans. mach

ARKANSAS

Arkansas & Ozarks B&B Route 1, Box 38 Calico Rock, AR 72519	501-297-8764 $ Dep. $20 Fr	Free Broch SASE Arkansas 6am-10pm
B&B Reservation Services Tourist Accomodations 11 Singleton Eureka Springs, AR 72632	501-253-9111 $ Dep. 1 night Visa, MC	Eureka Springs 24 hours

CALIFORNIA

B&B International 1181-B Solano Ave. Albany, CA 94706	415-525-4569 $ Dep. $25 Visa, MC, AmEx, DC Fr,Ger,It,Ch,Jap,Sp	Brochure SASE California 8:30-5 PST M-F 9-12 Sat
Eye Openers B&B Reserv. P.O. Box 694 Altadena, CA 91001	213-684-4428 $ Dep $25 Visa/MC Sp,Fr,Ger,Rus,Heb	List $1, SASE All of California M-Sat 9am-6pm
Digs West 8191 Crowley Circle Buena Park, CA 90621	714-739-1669 $ Dep. 1 night Fr,Ger,Sp	Brochure SASE CA, especially Southern CA 8:30am-5:30pm M-F or ans. machine
B&B Exchange 1458 Lincoln Ave. Suite 3 Calistoga, CA 94515	707-942-5900 800-654-2992 $$ Dep. 1 night Visa, MC Sw,Ger,Fin,Lith	Free Brochure California M-F 8:30am-6pm Sat 10a-12p, 2-6p
B&B Homestay P.O. Box 326 Cambria, CA 93428	805-927-4613 800-447-6667 $$ Full deposit Du,Ger,It	Free brochure CA Central Coast 24 hrs, 7 days

Carolyn's B&B Homes in San Diego 416 Third Ave. Chula Vista, CA 92010	619-422-7009 $ Dep. 50% Sp,Ger	Brochure SASE Southern CA M-F 9am-6pm
B&B of Southern California 1943 Sunny Crest Dr., Suite 304 Fullerton, CA 92635	714-738-8361 $ Dep. 20% Sp,Fr,Ger,Du,It,ASL	Brochure SASE California M-F 9am-5pm weekends
Mendocino Coast Reservations 1001 Main St., P.O. Box 1034 Mendocino, CA 95460	707-937-1913 $ Dep. 3 nights full Visa, MC	Free brochure California 9am-6pm 7 days
B&B Hospitality Res. Srvc. P.O. Box 2407 Oceanside, CA 92054	619-722-6694 $ Dep. 1 night, cash Sp,Heb,Ger,Fr,Jap	Free brochure California M-F 8am-6pm Sat 9-12 noon
B&B Exchange of Marin 45 Entrata Ave. San Anselmo, CA 94960	415-485-1971 $$ Dep. 1 night	Free brochure CA Marin County all hours
American Family Inn/B&B SF P.O. Box 349 San Francisco, CA 94101	415-931-3083 $$ Dep. 1 night or Visa, MC, AmEx Ger,Fr,Sp,Rus	Free brochure Listing $2 California 9:30am-5pm M-F
Hospitality Plus P.O. Box 388 San Juan Capistrano, CA 92693	714-496-7050 $ Dep. 1 night	Free brochure CA Beach Cities 9am-5pm
Megan's Friends B&B Reservations 1776 Royal Way San Luis Obispo, CA 93401	805-544-4406 $ Dep. 20% Aus,Ger,Dut	Brochure SASE California Central Coast 11am-4pm; 6-10pm Daily
California Houseguests Int'l. 18652 Ventura Blvd., #190-B Tarzana, CA 91356	818-344-7878 $ Dep. $25 All times OK Fr,Ger,Sp	Free Brochure CA, other states Canada, Mex, Eur answering machine prompt call back
CoHost, America's B&B P.O. Box 9302 Whittier, CA 90608	213-699-8427 $$ Dep. $25	Listing $3 California 7am-7pm 7 days

More RSO's...

Travelers B&B   P.O. Box 1368, Chino 91710   714-627-7971
Rent A Room B&B   11531 Varna St., Garden Grove 92640   714-638-1406
Seaview Reservations   P.O. Box 1355, Laguna Beach 92652   714-494-8878
B&B Reservation Service   1834 First St., Napa 94558   707-224-4667
El Camino Real B&B   P.O. Box 7155, Northridge 91327   818-363-6753

California B&B   P.O. Box 1551, Sacramento 95807
B&B Almanac   Box 295, Saint Helena 94574   707-963-0852
San Diego B&B   P.O. Box 178315, San Diego 92117   619-560-7322
Casita Blanca   330 Edgehill Way, San Francisco 94127   415-564-9339
Roomservice Inn Res.   330 Townsend St., Suite 113, San Francisco 94107   415-543-4522
University B&B   66 Clarendon Ave., San Francisco 94114   415-661-8940
American Historic Homes B&B   P.O. Box 388, San Juan Capistrano 92693   714-496-7050
B&B Laguna Beach   P.O. Box 388, San Juan Capistrano 92693   714-496-7050
Wine Country B&B   P.O. Box 3211, Santa Rosa 95403   707-578-1661
Mona's B&B Homes   P.O. Box 1805, Temecula 92390
B&B Approved Hosts Res/ Serv.   10890 Galvin, Ventura 93004   805-647-0651
B&B of Los Angeles   32074 Waterside Lane, Westlake Village 91361   818-889-7325
Accommodation Referral Reserv.   P.O. Box 2766, Yountville 94599   707-944-8891

COLORADO

B&B Colorado Ltd. P.O. Box 6061 Boulder, CO 80306	303-494-4994 $ Dep. 25% Visa, MC	Brochure $4 Colorado 9am-5pm M-F
B&B Rocky Mountains & Skiers P.O. Box 804 Colorado Springs, CO 80901	719-630-3433 $ Dep. 1 night skiers 50% Visa, MC	Directory $4.50 CO/NM/WY/MT/UT M-F 9am-5pm 12pm-5pm (wint.)
B&B Vail/Ski Areas P.O. Box 491 Vail, CO 81658	303-949-1212 $ Dep. 50-100% Visa, MC Ger,Sp	Brochure $2 CO ski areas nationally summer 1-6pm winter 9-6pm

More RSO's. . .

Historic Hotel Reservations   1540 S. Holly, Denver 80222   303-759-1918

CONNECTICUT

B&B Ltd. P.O. Box 216 New Haven, CT 06513	203-469-3260 $ Dep. 20% travelers checks Fr,Sp,Ger	List SASE Connecticut 5-9:30 school dys anytime summer
Covered Bridge B&B P.O. Box 447 Norfolk, CT 06058	203-542-5690 $$ Full deposit Visa, MC, AmEx	Free list SASE Connecticut 9am-6pm M-F
Alexander's B&B Res. Service Box 534 Salisbury, CT 06068	203-435-9539 $$ Dep. full amount Visa, MC	Brochure SASE Connecticut Mass., New York 9am-10pm daily

More RSO's. . .

Nautilus B&B   133 Phoenix Drive, Groton 06340   203-448-1538
Seacoast Landings   133 Neptune Drive, Groton 06340   203-442-1940

Nutmeg B&B   222 Girard Ave., Hartford 06105   203-236-6698
Four Seasons International   11 Bridlepath Rd., West Simsbury 06092   203-651

DELAWARE

B&B of Delaware	302-479-9500	Free Brochure
3650 Silverside Rd., Box 177	$$	DE, PA, MD
Wilmington, DE 19810	Dep. 20%	M-F 9am-9pm

FLORIDA

B&B of the Florida Keys	305-743-4118	Free Brochure
5 Man-O-War Drive	$	Florida Keys
Marathon, FL 33050	Dep. 1-2 nights	Florida E. Coast
	Ger	9am-5pm

Central Florida B&B	904-351-1167	Free brochure
719 SE 4th St.	$	Central Florida
Ocala, FL 32671	Dep. 20%	8a-5p 7 days

More RSO's...

Tropical Isles B&B   P.O. Box 490-382, Key Biscayne 33149   305-361-2937
B&B Company   1205 Mariposa Ave. #233, Miami 33146   305-661-3270
Magic B&B   8328 Curry Ford Rd., Orlando 32822   407-277-6602
Open House B&B Resgistry   P.O. Box 3025, Palm Beach 33480   305-842-5190
Florida & England B&B   P.O. Box 12, Palm Harbor 33563   813-784-5118
B&B Suncoast Accomm.   8690 Gulf Blvd., St. Pete Beach 33706   813-360-1753
Tallahassee B&B   3023 Windy Hill Lane, Tallahassee 32308   904-385-3768
A & A B&B of Florida   P.O. Box 1316, Winter Park 32790   305-628-3233

GEORGIA

B&B Atlanta	404-875-0525	Brochure SASE
1801 Piedmont Ave., N.E. #208	$	Georgia
Atlanta, GA 30324	Dep. 1 night	Metro Atlantic
	Visa, MC, AmEx	9-12, 2-5 M-F
	Heb,Fr,Ger,Yid	

R.S.V.P. Savannah B&B	912-232-7787	Free brochure
417 E. Charlton St.	$$	Georgia
Savannah, GA 31401	Dep. 1 night	9am-6pm daily
	Visa, MC, AmEx	
	personal check	

Savannah Historic Inns	912-233-7660	Free brochure
& Guest Houses	800-262-4667	Georgia
147 Bull St.	$40-135	9am-5pm M-F
Savannah, GA 31401	Dep. 1 night	
	Visa, MC, AmEx	

Quail Country B&B	912-226-7218	Free brochure
1104 Old Monticello Rd.	$	Thomasville, GA
Thomasville, GA 31792	Dep. $25	9am—9pm

More RSO's...

Atlanta Hospitality   2472 Lauderdale Dr., Atlanta 30345   404-493-1930
B&B Inns   117 West Gordon St., Savannah 31401   912-238-0518
Savannah Area Visitors Bureau   801 Broad St., Savannah 31499   912-236-1774

HAWAII

B&B Honolulu 3242 Kaohinani Dr. Honolulu, HI 96817	808-595-7533 800-288-4666 $ Dep. 3 days or 50%	Free brochure Hawaiian islands 8am-8pm exc. Sun.
B&B Pacific-Hawaii 19 Kai Nani Pl. Kailua, Oahu, HI 96734	808-262-6026 808-263-4848 $ Dep. 20-50%	Brochure $3 Hawwaii/Oahu/Maui Kauai, Worldwide 24 hours
B&B Hawaii P.O. Box 449 Kapaa, HI 96746	808-822-7771 $ Dep. 20% Ger,Fr,Hun,Swiss	Guide book $6 Hawaii all islands 8:30-4:30 M-F
B&B Maui Style P.O. Box 886 Kihei, Maui, HI 96753	808-878-7865 $ Dep. 20%	Free listing Hawaii 8am-9am & during day

IDAHO

B&B of Idaho P.O. Box 7323 Boise, ID 83707	208-336-5174 $ Dep. $20 Visa, MC	Directory SASE Idaho 9am-5pm M-F

More RSO's. . .

B&B Connections   5805 Pinegrove Dr. W, Coeur d'Alene 83814   208-765-9090

ILLINOIS

B&B/Chicago P.O. Box 14088 Chicago, IL 60614-0088	312-951-0085 $$ Dep. $25 Visa, MC, AmEx Fr,Sp,Assy,Per	Free brochure Downtown Chicago North Shore 9-5 M-F

More RSO's. . .

Heritage B&B   P.O. Box 60054, Chicago 60660   312-728-7935

INDIANA

More RSO's. . .

Amish Acres—Indiana Amish   1600 W Market St., Nappanee 46550   219-773-4188
InnServ Nationwide Reservation   Rt 1 Box 68, Redkey 47373   317-369-2245

IOWA

B&B in Iowa, Ltd. P.O. Box 340 Preston, IA 52069	319-689-4222 $ Dep. $20 or 1 night Ger,Fr	List $1 Iowa, USA Canada, Europe 7am-10pm Mon-Sat

More RSO's. . .

B&B—Quad Cities   Box 488, Davenport 52805   319-359-4156

KANSAS

B&B Kansas City P.O. Box 14781 Lenexa, KS 66215	913-888-3636 $ Dep. 20% + tax	Brochure SASE Missouri, Kansas 8am-11pm daily w/answering mach.

More RSO's...

Bed & Biscuits Home Lodging   P.O. Box 121, Harper 67058   316-896-7880

KENTUCKY

Ohio Valley B&B, Inc. 6876 Taylor Mill Rd. Independence, KY 41051	606-356-7865 $ Dep. 1 night Visa, MC, AmEx Discover	Brochure SASE Ohio, N. Kentucky S.E. Indiana 9am-9pm M-F
Kentucky Homes B&B, Inc. 1431 St. James Court Louisville, KY 40208	502-635-7341 $ Dep. $25 Visa, MC, AmEx It,Fr,Ger,Port	Brochure $1 Kentucky Southern Indiana M-F 8am-12pm
Bluegrass B&B Route 1, Box 263 Versailles, KY 40383	606-873-3208 $ Dep. 25% + tax	Free Brochure Kentucky 9am-9pm 7 days

LOUISIANA

B&B Reservation Services Worldwide P.O. Box 14797 Baton Rouge, LA 70898	504-346-1928	List of RSO's $3 Worldwide 9am-5pm M-F
Southern Comfort B&B 2856 Hundred Oaks Ave. Baton Rouge, LA 70808	504-346-1928 504-346-9815 $ Dep. $20 per night Visa, MC Fr,Sp,It	Directory $3 Louisiana 8am-8pm 7 days
New Orleans B&B P.O. Box 8163 New Orleans, LA 70182	504-822-5038 504-822-5046 $ Dep. 20% Visa, MC, AmEx Ger,Fr,Rus	Free brochure Louisiana 8am-4pm M-F

More RSO's...

B&B Inc.   1360 Moss St., Box 52257, New Orleans 70152   504-525-4640
Bed, Bath & Breakfast   Box 15843, 4431 St. Charles Ave., New Orleans 70175   504-897-3867

MAINE ───────────────────────────────

B&B of Maine
32 Colonial Village
Falmouth, ME 04105

207-781-4528
$
Dep. 1 night
Visa, MC
Fr,Sp,Ger

Print listing $1
Maine
Evenings/weekends
or ans. machine

More RSO's...

B&B Down East   Box 547, Macomber Mill Rd., Eastbrook 04634   207-565-3517
Nova Scotia Tourist Information   129 Commercial St., Portland 04101

MARYLAND ───────────────────────────

Traveller in Maryland, Inc.
P.O. Box 2277
Annapolis, MD 21404

301-269-6232
301-261-2233
$
Dep. 1 night
Visa, MC, AmEx

Maryland
UK
9-5 M-Th, 9-12n F

Amanda's B&B Reservation
1428 Park Ave.
Baltimore, MD 21217

301-225-0001
$$
Dep. 1 night
Visa, MC, AmEx
Fr,Ger,It,Arab

Brochure SASE
Maryland
8:30-5pm M-F

MASSACHUSETTS ───────────────────────

B&B Marblehead & Northshore
54 Amherst Road, P.O. Box 172
Beverly, MA 01915

508-921-1336
$
Dep. $25 per night
Visa, MC, AmEx

Free Brochure
Directory $3.50
Boston, Cape Cod
NH, ME, VT
Mon-Sat

B&B Agency of Boston
47 Commercial Wharf
Boston, MA 02110

617-720-3540
$$
Dep. 30%
Visa, MC
Fr,Sp,Ger,Arab,It

Free Brochure
Massachusetts
8am-11pm daily

B&B Associates Bay Colony
P.O. Box 57166, Babson Park
Boston, MA 02157-0166

617-449-5302
$$
Dep 30%
Visa, MC, AmEx
Fr,Ger,It,Nor,Sp,Gr

Brochure $3.75
Massachusetts
10-12:30 &
10am-5pm M-F

Host Homes of Boston
P.O. Box 117, Waban Branch
Boston, MA 02168

617-244-1308
$
Dep. 1 night
Visa, MC, AmEx
Fr,Ger,Sp,Gr,Jap,Ru

Free brochure
MA, Boston, Cape
Cod, Marblehead
M-F 9:30am-12pm,
1:30pm-4:30 am

Folkestone B&B
P.O. Box 931
Boylston, MA 01505- 0931

617-869-2687
$$
Dep. 1 night
Visa, MC

Brochure SASE
Central MA
10-5 or ans. mch.

Greater Boston Hospitality P.O. Box 1142 Brookline, MA 02146	617-277-5430 $$ Dep. 50% of total Visa, MC Sp,Fr,Heb,Ger,It	Brochure $3.50 Massachusetts 8am-5:30pm M-F ½ day Saturday
B&B Cambridge & Greater Boston P.O. Box 665 Cambridge, MA 02140	617-576-1492 617-576-2112 $$ Dep. 30% Visa, MC, AmEx	Free brochure Cambridge & Greater Boston 9a-6p M-F 2p-6p Sat
Pineapple Hospitality, Inc. 47 N. 2nd St., Suite 3A New Bedford, MA 02740	508-990-1696 $$ Dep. $15 per night Visa, MC, AmEx French, German	Brochure $5.95 CT,RI,MA,VT,NH,ME Bermuda 9am-5pm M-F
House Guests Cape Cod & Isl. Box 1881 Orleans, MA 02653	800-666-HOST 617-896-7053 $ Dep. 50% Visa, MC, AmEx	Listing $3 Cape Cod, Nantuck Martha's Vineyard 8am-8pm daily
Be Our Guest, B&B, Ltd. P.O. Box 1333 Plymouth, MA 02066	617-837-9867 $ Dep $25 Visa, MC, AmEx Fr	Free brochure Massachusetts 10am-8pm 7 days
B&B/The National Network Box 4616 Springfield, MA 01101	$ Dep. 1 night Visa, MC	Free Broch. SASE all 50 states
B&B Cape Cod P.O. Box 341 West Hyannisport, MA 02672	508-775-2772 $ Dep 25% Visa, MC, AmEx	Free brochure Massachusetts Cape Cod & islnds 8:30-7:30 M-Sat
Berkshire Bed & Breakfast P.O. Box 211 Williamsburg, MA 01096	$	

More RSO's. . .

B&B Brookline/Boston   Box 732, Brookline 02146   617-277-2292
B&B in Minuteman Country DUPLIC   P.O. Box 665, Cambridge 02140   617-576-2112
B&B, House Guests, Cape Cod   Box AR, Dennis 02638   617-398-0787
B&B in Minuteman Country   8 Carriage Drive, Lexington 02173   617-861-7063
Marshall House Christian Hosp.   P.O. Box 2124, Lynn 01902   617-595-6544
Educators Inn   P.O. Box 663, Lynnfield 01940   617-334-6144
New England B&B   1045 Centre St., Newton Centre 02159   617-244-2112
Orleans B&B Associates   P.O. Box 1312, Orleans 02653   617-255-3824
Around Plymouth Bay, Inc. B&B   P.O. Box 6211, Plymouth 02360   617-747-5075
B&B in New England   Main Street, Williamsburg 01096-0211   413-268-7244

MICHIGAN

B&B in Michigan P.O. Box 1731 Dearborn, MI 48121	313-561-6041 $ Dep. $25 minimum Visa, MC Ger	Brochure SASE Michigan 6-10pm M-F
Go Native. . . Hawaii P.O. Box 13115 Lansing, MI 48901	517-349-9598 $ Dep 60% Ger,Sp,Sw,Jap,Kor	Free brochure Directory $2 Hawaiian Islands 24 hr/ans. mach.

More RSO's. . .

Frankenmuth Area B&B   337 Trinklein St., Frankenmuth 48734   517-652-8897
B&B of Grand Rapids   344 College S.E., Grand Rapids 49503   616-451-4849

MINNESOTA

More RSO's. . .

B&B Registry Ltd.   P.O. Box 8174, Saint Paul 55108   612-646-4238

MISSISSIPPI

Lincoln Ltd. B&B P.O. Box 3479, 2303-23rd Ave. Meridian, MS 39303	601-482-5483 $ Dep. 1 night Visa, MC Fr,Ger	List $3.00 Broch free SASE MS, AL, TN, LA 9-5 M-F
Creative Travel B&B Center Canal Street Depot Natchez, MS 39120	800-824-0355 $ Dep. 1 night Visa, MC	Free brochure Mississippi Louisiana M-F 9am-5pm
Natchez Pilgrimage Tours P.O. Box 347 Natchez, MS 39121	601-446-6631 800-647-6742 $$ Visa, MC, AmEx	Free brochure Mississippi only Natchez 8:30am-5:00pm

MISSOURI

Ozark Mountain Country B&B Box 295-IG Branson, MO 65616	417-334-5077 417-334-4720 $ Visa, MC Dep. 1 night plus $20 each add'l.	Free list SASE SW Missouri NW Ark., Nebraska 7am-11pm 7 days
B&B St. Louis 11005 Manchester Rd. Saint Louis, MO 63122	314-533-9299 $ Visa, MC	Free list St.Lou & sbrb are 8am-5pm & some ev

More RSO's. . .

Truman Country B&B   424 N. Pleasant, Independence 64050   816-254-6657
Midwest Host B&B   P.O. Box 27, Saginaw 64846   417-782-9112
River Country of Mo. & Ill.   #1 Grandview Hts., Saint Louis 63131   314-965-4328

MONTANA ────────────────────────────

B&B Western Adventure	406-259-7993	Free Brochure
P.O. Box 20972	$	Directory $4.50
Billings, MT 59102-0972	Dep. 1 night or 25%	Montana, Wyoming
	Visa, MC	M-F 9-5 summer
		1-5 winter

More RSO's...

Western B&B Hosts   P.O. Box 322, Kalispell 59901   406-257-4476

NEBRASKA ────────────────────────────

B&B of the Great Plains	402-423-3480	Free list SASE
P.O. Box 2333	$	Nebraska, Iowa
Lincoln, NE 68502	Dep. 20% + tax	24 hr ans mach
	Visa, MC, AmEx	

More RSO's...

Swede Hospitality B&B   1617 Avenue A, Gothenburg 69138   308-537-2680

NEW HAMPSHIRE ──────────────────────

More RSO's...

New Hampshire B&B   RFD 3, Box 53, Laconia 03246   603-279-8348
Valley B&B   Box 1190, North Conway 03860   207-935-3799

NEW JERSEY ───────────────────────────

B&B of New Jersey	201-444-7409	Brochure SASE
Suite 132	$	Entire US/Int'l.
103 Godwin Ave.#1 night dep.		9am—4pm M-F
Midland Park, NJ 07432		

B&B of Princeton	609-924-3189	Letter & Res.form
P.O. Box 571	$$	Princeton
Princeton, NJ 08540	Dep. 1 night	24 hr ans machine

More RSO's...

Town & Country B&B   P O Box 301, Lambertville 08350   609-397-8399

NEW MEXICO ───────────────────────────

B&B of Santa Fe	505-982-3332	Brochure SASE
625 Don Felix	$$	Santa Fe, Taos
Santa Fe, NM 87501	Full dep.	9am-5pm M-Sat

NEW YORK ─────────────────────────────

B&B USA Ltd.	914-271-6228	List $4
129 Grand St.	$	New York
Croton-on-Hudson, NY 10520	Dep 50% or 1 night	M-F 9am-3pm
	Visa, MC	
	Fr,Ger,Jap,Rom,Heb	

Hampton Bed & Breakfast P.O. Box 378 East Moriches, NY 11940	516-878-8197 $$$ Dep. 1 night	Brochure SASE New York 7 days-machine
B&B Rochester P.O. Box 444 Fairport, NY 14450	716-223-8877 $ Dep. 1 night	Brochure SASE Rochester & Finger Lakes area 1pm-6pm Tu- Th
B&B Leatherstocking 389 Brockway Rd. Frankfort, NY 13340	315-733-0040 $ Dep. 50% 1st night Visa, MC Fr,Sp,Ger	Free Brochure Directory $2 Central New York 7am-10pm Daily
North Country B&B Res. Serv. P.O. Box 286 Lake Placid, NY 12946	518-523-9474 $ Dep. 1 night	Free brochure Adirondacks, NY 10am-10pm daily
...Aaah! B&B #1, Ltd. P.O. Box 200 New York, NY 10108	212-246-4000 $$ Dep. 25% AmEx	Free brochure New York City 9am-5pm M-F 10am-2pm Sat
Abode B&B Ltd. P.O. Box 20022 New York, NY 10028	212-472-2000 $$ Dep. 25%	Free brochure NY, Manhattan Brooklyn Heights 9am-5pm M-F, 10am-2pm Sat, mach.
B&B (& Books) 35 W. 92nd St. New York, NY 10025	212-865-8740 $$ Dep. 20%-25% Fr,Ger	Free list SASE Manhattan M-F 9am-3pm
B&B Network of New York 134 W. 32nd St. Suite 602 New York, NY 10001	212-645-8134 $$ Dep. 25%	Free brochure New York 8am-6pm M-F
New World B&B 150 5th Ave. #711 New York, NY 10011	212-675-5600 800-443-3800 exNY $$ Dep. 25% Visa, MC, AmEx	Free brochure Manhattan 9am-5pm M-F
Urban Ventures, Inc. P.O. Box 426 New York, NY 10024	212-594-5650 FAX 212-947-9320 $$ Dep. 1 night Visa, MC, AmEx	Free list SASE New York City England 9-5 M-F, 9-3 Sat
American Country Collection 984 Gloucester Place Schenectady, NY 12309	518-370-4948 $ Dep 50% or 1 night Visa, MC, AmEx Fr,Sp,Ch	Free Brochure Directory $2 New York, Vt. W. Massachusetts M-F 10-12, 1-5

B&B of Greater Syracuse	315-446-4199	Free broch. SASE
143 Didama St.	$	New York-Central
Syracuse, NY 13224	Dep. 1 night or	Finger Lakes
	50% entire stay	daily by resv.

More RSO's...

Alternative Lodging   P.O. Box 1782, East Hampton 11937   516-324-9449
Mid-Island B&B Reservation   518 Mid-Island Plaza, Hicksville 11801   516-931-1234
Cherry Valley Ventures   6119 Cherry Valley Trnpk., Lafayette 13084   315-677-9723
B&B Group (NY'ers at Home)   301 E. 60th Street, New York 10022   212-838-7015
Puerto Rico Tourist Co.   1290 Avenue of Americas, New York 10104
U.S. Virgin Isl. Gov't Travel   1270 Avenue of Americas, New York 10020
Rainbow Hospitality   9348 Hennepin Avenue, Niagara Falls 14304   716-283-4794
Island B&B Registry   5 Exeter Court, Northport 11768   516-757-7398
Bed & Breakfast of Long Island   Box 392, Old Westbury 11568   516-334-6231
Bed-N-Breakfast Reservation   P O Box 1015, Pearl River 10965   914-735-4857
A Reasonable Alternative, Inc.   117 Spring St. Suite 100, Port Jefferson 11777   516-928-4034
Tobin's B&B Guide   Rd. 2, Box 64, Rhinebeck 12572
B&B of Columbia County   Box 122, Spencertown 12165   518-392-2358

NORTH CAROLINA ───────────────

More RSO's...

Charlotte B&B   1700-2 Delane Ave., Charlotte 28211   704-366-0979
B&B in the Albemarle   P.O. Box 248, Everetts 27825   919-792-4584

OHIO ──────────────────────

Private Lodgings, Inc.	216-321-3213	Free brochure
P.O. Box 18590	$	Ohio
Cleveland, OH 44118	Full deposit	9-12n, 3-5pm M-F
	Ger,Fr,Yid	

More RSO's...

Columbus B&B   769 S. 3rd St., Columbus 43206   614-443-3680
Buckeye B&B   P.O. Box 130, Powell 43065   614-548-4555

OKLAHOMA ──────────────────

More RSO's...

Redbud Reserv. B&B for OK   P O Box 23954, Oklahoma City 73123   405-720-0212

OREGON ─────────────────────

Country Host Registry	503-863-5168	Free brochure
901 NW Chadwick Lane	$	9am-9pm
Myrtle Creek, OR 97457	Visa confirm.	
	Visa, MC	

Northwest B&B Travel Unltd.	503-243-7616	Free Brochure
610 SW Broadway	$	Directory $8
Portland, OR 97205	No dep. required	No'west, HI, CA
	Fr,Ger,It,Sp,Du,Heb	Canada BC
		M-F 9am-5pm

More RSO's...

Roomservice   No business by mail, Ashland   503-488-0338
Gallucci Hosts Hostels B&B   P.O. Box 1303, Lake Oswego 97035   503-636-6933
B&B Accomod.—Oregon Plus   5733 S.W. Dickinson St., Portland 97219   503-245-0642
P T International   1318 S.W. Troy St., Portland 97219   800-547-1463

PENNSYLVANIA

B&B of Philadelphia P.O. Box 630 Chester Springs, PA 19425	215-827-9650 $ Dep. 1 night Visa, MC	Free descr SASE Phila & surround- ing counties 9-5 M-F, 12-4 Sat
B&B Connections P.O. Box 21 Devon, PA 19333	215-687-3565 $ Dep. 1 night or 20% Visa, MC, AmEx	Free sample dir. Philadephia & suburbs M-Sat 9am-9pm Sun 1pm-9pm
B&B—The Manor P.O. Box 656 Havertown, PA 19083	215-642-1323 $ Dep. 1 night Visa, MC	Brochure SASE Pennsylvania 9am-9pm daily
B&B of Chester County P.O. Box 825 Kennett Square, PA 19348	215-444-1367 $ Dep 20% Fr,Sp,Du,Ger,Ital	List $3 SASE PA/DE 4pm-9pm
Pittsburgh B&B 2190 Ben Franklin Dr. Pittsburgh, PA 15237	412-367-8080 $ Dep. $20 or 20% Visa, MC Sp,Fr	Free broch. SASE Pennsylvania 9-5 M-F 9-12 wknd
B&B of Valley Forge P.O. Box 562 Valley Forge, PA 19481	215-783-7838 $ Dep. $25 minimum Visa, MC, AmEx Sp,Fr,It,Du,Ger	Free broch. SASE Pennsylvania all year 9am-11pm
Guesthouses, Inc Box 2137 West Chester, PA 19380	215-692-4575 $$ Dep. 20% + tax Visa, MC, AmEx Fr	Free Brochure PA/DE/NJ/MD Noon-4pm M-F RES. 24-hr ans machine

More RSO's...

B&B of Southeast Penn.   RD 1, Barto 19504   215-845-3526
Clarion County Tourism Agency   Court House, Clarion 16214   814-226-5001
B&B of Philadelphia   P.O. Box 680, Devon 19333-0680   215-688-1633
B&B Center City   1804 Pine St., Philadelphia 19103   215-735-1137
Rest & Repast B&B Service   P.O. Box 126, Pine Grove Mills 16868   814-238-1484

RHODE ISLAND ——————————————————————

Anna's Victorian Connection 5 Fowler Ave. Newport, RI 02840	401-849-2489 $$ Dep. 1 night Visa, MC, AmEx En Route; French	Free Brochure Rhode Island 24 hr. year round
B&B of Rhode Island P.O. Box 3292 38 Bellevue Ave. Newport, RI 02840	401-849-1298 $ Dep 1 nt + ½ bal Visa, MC, AmEx Fr,Ger,It,Malay	Free Broch SASE Directory $3 Rhode Island 9-5 M-F, plus 10-2 summer Sats.
Guest House Assoc. of Newport P.O. Box 981 Newport, RI 02840	401-846-ROOM $$ Dep. 50% full amt. Visa, MC, AmEx	Brochure SASE Rhode Island 24 hours
Newport Reservation Service P.O. Box 518 Newport, RI 02840	401-847-8878 $$ Deposit required Visa, MC, AmEx	Rhode Island M-F 9-4

More RSO's...

B&B, Newport   33 Russell Ave., Newport 02840   401-846-5408

SOUTH CAROLINA ——————————————————————

Charleston Society B&B 84 Murray Blvd. Charleston, SC 29401	803-723-4948 $$$ Dep. 1 night	Free Brochure Charleston 9am-5pm M-F
Historic Charleston B&B 43 Legare St. Charleston, SC 29401	803-722-6606 $$ Dep. 1 night Visa, MC, A,Ex Fr,Sp	Free brochure South Carolina Savanah, GA M-F 9:30-6 Fb-My 1pm-6 Ju-Sp,Nv-Jn
Charleston East B&B League 1031 Tall Pine Rd. Mount Pleasant, SC 29464	803-884-8208 $ Dep. 20%	Free Broch SASE South Carolina 10am-6pm, ans. mach. other times

SOUTH DAKOTA ——————————————————————

South Dakota B&B P.O. Box 90137 Sioux Falls, SD 57105	605-339-0759 605-528-6571 $ Dep. $20	Free Brochure South Dakota Mon-Sun after 5pm

More RSO's...

Old West & Badlands B&B Assoc.   P.O. Box 728, Philip 57567   605-859-2040

TENNESSEE

B&B in Memphis	901-726-5920	Brochure SASE
P.O. Box 41621	$	Memphis
Memphis, TN 38174-621	Full payment	the mid-South
	Visa, MC	8:30am-6pm M-F
	Fr,Sp	1-5 Sat & Sun

B&B Host Homes of Tennessee	615-331-5244	Free Broch SASE
P.O. Box 110227	800-528-8433 270	TN, KY, FL,
Nashville, TN 37222	$	& international
	Full amount	9-5 M-F
	Visa, MC, AmEx	
	Sp,Fr,Ger	

More RSO's. . .

Jonesborough B&B   P.O. Box 722, Jonesborough 37659   615-753-9223
B&B of Nashville   P.O. Box 150651, Nashville 37215   615-298-5674

TEXAS

B&B Texas Style, Inc.	214-298-8586	Free Broch SASE
4224 W. Red Bird Lane	$	Directory $3
Dallas, TX 75237	Dep. 1 night or $20	Texas
	Visa, MC	9-5 M-F
	Fr,Ger,Sp,It	ans. mach. wkends

B&B of Fredericksburg	512-997-4712	Brochure $2
102 Cherry St.	$$	Texas
Fredericksburg, TX 78624	Dep. credit card #	9am-9pm daily
	Visa, MC	

Gasthaus Schmidt	512-997-5612	Free brochure
501 W. Main	Dep. 1 night	Fredericksburg,TX
Fredericksburg, TX 78624	or credit card	10am-5pm M-F
	Visa, MC, Amex	1pm-5pm Sat

More RSO's. . .

Sand Dollar Hospitality   3605 Mendenhall Dr., Corpus Christi 78415   512-853-1222
B&B Society Int'l   407 Cora St., Frederichsburg 78624   512-997-7150
B&B Society of Texas   921 Heights Blvd., Houston 77008   713-868-4654
B&B Hosts of San Antonio   166 Rockhill, San Antonio 78209   512-824-8036
B&B of Wimberley Texas   P.O. Box 589, Wimberley 78676   512-847-9666

UTAH

More RSO's. . .

B&B Assoc. of Utah   P.O. Box 16465, Salt Lake City 84116   801-532-7076

VERMONT

More RSO's. . .

Vermont Travel Infor. Serv.   Pond Village, Brookfield 05036   802-276-3120
Vermont B&B   P.O. Box 1, East Fairfield 05448   802-827-3827
American B&B in New England   Box 983, Saint Albans 05478

VIRGINA ————————————————————————————————

Princely B&B Ltd. 819 Prince Street Alexandria, VA 22314	703-683-2159 $$ Dep. 1 night Fr,Sp,Ger	Alexandria 10-6 M-F
Guesthouses B&B P.O. Box 5737 Charlottesville, VA 22905	804-979-7264 $ Dep 25% Visa MC AE Fr,Ger	List $1 SASE Charlottesville Luray, Albemarle 12pm-5pm M-F
B&B of Tidewater Virginia P.O. Box 3343 Norfolk, VA 23514	804-627-1983 $ Dep 20%	Free Brochure VA, coastal area year round or answering machine
Bensonhouse 2036 Monument Ave. Richmond, VA 23220	804-648-7560 $ Dep. 30% Visa, MC, AmEx	List $2 SASE Richmnd/Wllmsburg Fredericksburg 10-6 M-F wkend hrs vary
Travel Tree P.O. Box 838 Williamsburg, VA 23187	804-253-1571 $ Dep. $20	Free Brochure Williamsburg 6-9pm Mon-Thur

More RSO's. . .

Blue Ridge B&B Reserv.   Rocks & Rills Farm, Rt 2 Bx 3895, Berryville 22611   703-955-1246
Shenandoah Valley   P.O. Box 305, Broadway 22815   703-896-9702
Rockbridge Reservations   Sleepy Hollow, Box 76, Brownsburg 24415   703-348-5698
Sojourners B&B   P.O. Box 3587, Lynchburg 24503   804-384-1655
B&B on the Hill   2304 East Broad Street, Richmond 23223   804-780-3746
Commissioned Host & Toast   P.O. Box 2177, Springfield 22152   703-768-5858

WASHINGTON ————————————————————————————————

Pacific B&B Agency 701 N.W. 60th St. Seattle, WA 98107	206-784-0539 $ Dep. $25 Visa, MC, AmEx Ger,Fr,Dan,Nor,Du	Free Brochure Sample $2 SASE Washington British Columbia 9-5 M-F Ans Mach.

More RSO's. . .

B&B Service (BABS)   400 W.Lake Samish Dr. POB 5025, Bellingham 98227   206-733-8642
RSVP B&B Reserv. Station   P.O. Box 778, Ferndale 98248   206-384-6586
Whidbey Island B&B Assoc.   P.O. Box 259, Langley 98260   206-321-6272
Methow Valley Central Reserv.   P.O. Box 253, Mazama 98833   509-996-2148
Travellers' B&B   P.O. Box 492, Mercer Island 98040   206-232-2345
Seattle B&B Inn Assoc.   P.O. Box 95853, Seattle 98145   206-547-1020
INNterlodging Co-op Services   P.O. Box 7044, Tacoma 98407   206-756-0343

WASHINGTON DC

B&B League, Ltd.	202-363-7767	Free broch SASE
3639 Van Ness St. NW	$	DC and suburbs
Washington, DC 20008	Dep. $25	9-5 M-Th/9-1 Fri
	Visa, MC, AmEx	

Bed 'n' Breakfast Ltd.	202-328-3510	Free Brochure
P.O. Box 12011	$	Washington, D.C.
Washington, DC 20005	Dep $40	metropolitan area
	Visa, MC, AmEx	10am-5pm M-F
	Fr,Sp	10-1 Sat

More RSO's...

Sweet Dreams & Toast, Inc.   P.O. Box 4835-0035, Washington 20008   202-483-9191

WEST VIRGINA

More RSO's...

Countryside Accommodations   Box 57, Summit Point 25446   304-725-2614

WISCONSIN

B&B Guest Homes	414-743-9742	Free broch SASE
Route 2, 698 Country U	$	Wisconsin
Algoma, WI 54201	Dep. 1 night	Door County
	Visa, MC	Wisconsin
	Swe,Nor,Ger,Kor	6am-9pm daily

B&B of Milwaukee, Inc.	414-271-2337	Free Broch SASE
320 E. Buffalo St.	$	Wisconsin
Milwaukee, WI 53202	Full amt dep.	9-5 M-F
	Visa/MC	ans. mach. 24 hrs
	Sp,Fr,Port	

More RSO's...

B&B Information Service   458 Glenway St., Madison 53711   608-238-6776

ALBERTA

More RSO's...

B&B Bur. Canadian Care   POB 7094, Post Sta. E, Calgary T3C 3L8   403-242-5555
Alberta Hostelling Assoc.   10926 88th Ave., Edmonton T6G 0Z1   403-433-5513
Big Country B&B   P.O. Box 714, Rosebud T0J 2T0   403-677-2269

BRITISH COLUMBIA

Born Free B&B of B.C. Ltd.	604-298-8815	Free brochure
4390 Frances St.	$$	Greater Vancouver
Burnaby, BC V5C 2R3	Dep. 1 night	Victoria
	Visa, MC	9-5 + Ans. serv.
	Dut,Ger,It,Fr	

Vancouver B&B Ltd.	604-291-6147	Free Brochure
1685 Ingleton Ave.	$$	Greater Vancouver
Burnaby, BC V5C 4L8	Dep 20% or 1 night	8:30-4:30 M-F
	Visa	ans mach aft hrs
	Fr,Sp,Jap,Pol	

Old English B&B Registry	604-986-5069	Free Brochure
P.O. Box 86818	$	Vancouver
North Vancouver, BC V7L 4L3	Dep. 1 night	11-4pm & ans mach
	Visa, MC	will return calls

AB&C B&B of Vancouver	604-263-5595	
P.O. Box 66109, Stn F	$$	Vancouver, BC
Vancouver, BC	Dep. 25%	9am-5pm M-F or
	Visa, MC	ans machine

First Choice B&B Agency	604-875-8888	Free brochure
658 E. 29th Ave.	$	British Columbia
Vancouver, BC V5V 2R9	Dep. 1 night	24 hours
	Visa, MC	

Town & Country B&B in B.C.	604-731-5942	Free Brochure
P.O. Box 46544, Stn. G	$$	Guide $9.95
Vancouver, BC V6R 4G6	Dep. 1-2 nights	British Columbia
	Fr,Ger,Sp	8am-5pm M-F
		evening & wkends

All Season B&B Agency	604-595-2337	Free Brochure
Box 5511, Stn. B	604-595-BEDS	Book $6
Victoria, BC V8R 6S4	$	British Columbia
	Dep. 20%	9am-5pm M-F
	Fr,Du,Ger	early/later wkend

Garden City B&B	604-479-9999	Free brochure
660 Jones Terrace	$40-100	Victoria/Gulf &
Victoria, BC V8Z 2L7	Dep. 1 night	Vancouver Islands
	Visa, MC, AmEx	8am-10pm daily
	Fr,Ger,Sp,Dan,Jap	

More RSO's...

Royal West B&B Registry 8041 Alexandra Rd., Richmond V6X 1C3 604-276-2144
Alberta B&B POB 15477, Main P.O., Vancouver V6B 5B2 604-682-4610
Traveller's B&B 1840 Midgard Ave., Victoria V8P 2Y9 604-477-3069
VIP B&B 1786 Teakwood Road, Victoria V8N 1E2 604-477-5604
Host International B&B 2695 Lawson Ave., W. Vancouver V7V 2G3 604-926-0004

MANITOBA ──────

B&B of Manitoba	204-256-6151	Brochure $1
93 Healey Crescent	$	Manitoba
Winnipeg, MB R2N 2S2	Dep. 1 night	9am-5pm
	Ger,Pol,Ukr	

NEW BRUNSWICK ──────

More RSO's...

New Brunswick Tourism P.O. Box 12345, Frederick E3B 5C3

NEWFOUNDLAND ──────

More RSO's...

Tourist Services Division Box 2061, Saint John's A1C 5R8

ONTARIO

Serena's Place 720 Headley Dr. London, ON N6H 3V6	519-471-6228 $	Brochure $1 SASE Ontario 8am-6pm
Niagara Region B&B Service 2631 Dorchester Rd. Niagara Falls, ON L2J 2Y9	416-358-8988 $$ Dep. $25 Visa, MC, AmEx Ger,Pol,Ukr,Fr	Free brochure Ontario Niagara Peninsula 9am-9pm daily
Ottawa Area B&B Box 4848 Station E Ottawa, ON K1S 5J1	613-563-0161 $ Dep. 1 night Fr,Sp,Ger	Free brochure Ontario 10am-10pm daily
Downtown Toronto Assoc. of B&B 153 Huron St. Toronto, ON M5T 2B6	416-977-6841 416-598-4562 $$ Dep. 50% Sp,It,Fr	Free brochure Toronto 9am-1pm daily ans mach 24 hrs
Toronto B&B (1987), Inc. Box 269, 253 College St. Toronto, ON M5T 1R5	416-961-3676 $ Dep. 50% Visa, MC Fr,Ger,It,Pol,Jap	Free brochure Metropltn Toronto Niagara-on-the-Lk 9am-6pm M-F

More RSO's. . .

Alma/Elmira/Elora B&B Assoc.   Washa Farm RR #2, Alma N0B 1A0   519-846-9788
Beachburg & Area B&B Assoc.   Box 146, Beachburg K0J 1C0   613-582-3585
B&B Prince Edward County   P.O. Box 160, Bloomfield K0K 1G0   613-393-3046
Brighton Area B&B Assoc.   61 Simpson St. Box 1106, Brighton K0K 1H0   613-475-0538
B&B Burlington   5435 Stratton Rd., Burlington L7L 2Z1   416-637-0329
So. Renfrew County B&B Ass'n.   c/o B. Collins POB 67, Calabogie K0J 1H0   613-752-2201
E. Ontario Country B&B   c/o Roduner Farm RR1, Cardinal K0E 1E0   613-657-4830
Seaway Valley B&B Assoc.   P.O. Box 884, Cornwall K6J 1Z3   613-932-0299
Ontario Assoc. of Accr.   Wyndham Hall RR1, Elmira N3B 2Z1   519-669-2379
Fergus/Elora B&B Assoc.   550 Saint Andrew St. E, Fergus N1M 1R6   519-843-2747
Flesherton & Beaver Valley   Box 119, Flesherton N0C 1E0   519-924-2675
Bonnechere B&B Assoc.   c/o Golden Gables Guests RR2, Golden Lake K0J 1X0
   613-625-2314
Muskoka B&B Assoc.   Box 1431, Gravenhurst P0C 1G0   705-687-4395
Hamilton-Wentworth B&B Assoc.   61 E 43rd St., Hamilton L8T 3B7   416-648-0461
Orillia & Area B&B Assoc.   c/o E. Laity, Hawkestone L0L 1T0   705-487-3135
B&B Kingston Area   10 Westview Rd., Kingston K7M 2C3   613-542-0214
Home Suite Home B&B   115 Erie St. S, Leamington N8H 3B5   519-326-7169
SW Ontario Countryside   c/o E.A. Henderson RR #1, Millbank N0K 1L0   519-595-4604
All Seasons B&B Assoc.   383 Mississauga Valley Blvd., Mississauga L5A 1Y9   416-276-4572
Durham East B&B Assoc.   c/o K. Brown RR2, Newcastle L0A 1H0   416-987-4096
Niagara-on-the-Lake B&B   P.O. Box 1515, Niagara-on-the-Lake L0S 1J0   416-358-8988
Capital B&B Assoc. Ottawa   2071 Riverside Dr., Ottawa K1H 7X2   613-737-4129
Country Host—Year Round   RR #1, Palgrave L0N 1P0   519-941-7633
Parry Sound & Dist. B&B   P.O. Box 71, Parry Sound P2A 2X2   705-342-9266
Pelee Island B&B Assoc.   c/o Lynn Tiessen, Pelee Island N0R 1M0   519-724-2068
Penetanguishene Area B&B Ass'n.   C.P. 1270, 63 rue Main, Penetanguishene L0K 1P0
   705-549-3116

B&B Prince Edward County   Box 1500, Picton K0K 2T0   613-476-6798
Grey Bruce B&B Assoc.   Box 1233, Port Elgin N0H 2T0   519-832-5520
Port Stanley & Sparta Area   324 Smith St. Box 852, Port Stanley N0L 2A0   519-782-4173
St. Catharines B&B Assoc.   489 Carlton St., Saint Catharines L2M 4W9   416-937-2422
Sarnia-Lambton B&B   #503-201 Front St. N, Sarnia N7T 7T9   519-332-1820
Thunder Bay Area B&B Assoc.   c/o The Unicorn Inn RR #1, South Gillies P0T 2V0
   807-577-1034
Stratford Area Visitors Bur.   38 Albert St., Stratford N5A 3K3   519-271-5140
Stratford B&B Two   208 Church St., Stratford N5A 2R6   519-273-4840
B&B Cornwall Area   P.O. Box 17 RR1, Summerstown K0C 2E0   613-931-2042
Metropolitan B&B Registry   72 Lowther Ave., Toronto M5R 1C8   416-964-2566
Prince Edward County B&B   299 Main St., Wellington K0K 3L0   613-399-2569

PRINCE EDWARD ISLAND

More RSO's. . .

Visitors Services Div.   P.O. Box 940, Charlottetown C1A 7MJ
Kensington Area Tourist Assoc.   RR 1, Kensington C0B 1M0   902-436-6847

QUEBEC

B&B Montreal 4912 Victoria Montreal, PQ H3W 2N1	514-738-9410 $ Dep $15 per night Visa/MC/AmEx Fr,Ger,Du,Slavic	Free Brochure Quebec Province 8:30am-8pm daily
B&B Network Hospitality 3977 Ave Laval Montreal, PQ H2W 2H9	514-287-9635 $$ Dep. 1 night Visa, MC	Montreal 8am-6pm
Downtown B&B Network 3458 Laval Ave. Montreal, PQ H2X 3C8	514-289-9749 $ Dep $15 Visa MC AE Fr,Ger,Sp,Ch,Viet	Free Brochure Montreal, Quebec 8am-10pm June-Aug 8-6 rest of year

More RSO's. . .

Bed & Breakfast de Chez Naus   5386 Brodeur Ave., Montreal H4A 1J3   514-485-1252
Mont—Royal Chez Soi, Inc.   5151 Cote-St.-Antoine, Montreal H4A 1P1
B&B Bonjour Quebec   3765, Bd. Monaco, Quebec G1P 3J3   418-527-1465
Tourism Quebec   CP 20 000, Quebec G1K 7X2
Gite Quebec   3729 Ave. le Corbusier, St-Foy G1W 4R8   418-651-1860

SASKATCHEWAN

More RSO's. . .

Saskatchewan Country Vacations   Box 89, Blaine Lake S0J 0J0   306-497-2782

YUKON

More RSO's. . .

Northern Network of B&B's   39 Donjek Rd., Whitehorse Y1A 3R1   403-667-4315
Tourism Yukon   Box 2703, Whitehorse Y1A 2C6
Yukon B&B   102-302 Steele St., Whitehorse Y1A 2C5   **403-668-2999**

B&B Inns with Special Amenities

Antiques

Many of the inns we list are graced by antiques. These inns have put a special emphasis on antiques and period decor.

Magic Canyon Ranch
Homer, AK

Greenway House
Bisbee, AZ

Happy Landing Inn
Carmel, CA

City Hotel
Columbia, CA

Carter House
Eureka, CA

Gingerbread Mansion
Ferndale, CA

Eastlake Inn
Los Angeles, CA

Meadow Creek Ranch
Mariposa, CA

Whitegate Inn
Mendocino, CA

**Maison Bleue Country
French B&B**
Pacific Grove, CA

Driver Mansion Inn
Sacramento, CA

Heritage Park B&B Inn
San Diego, CA

Monte Cristo
San Francisco, CA

Blue Quail Inn & Cottages
Santa Barbara, CA

Old Yacht Club Inn
Santa Barbara, CA

Trojan Horse Inn
Sonoma, CA

Wick's
Yuba City, CA

Holden House—1902
Colorado Springs, CO

Manor House
Norfolk, CT

Captain Stannard House
Westbrook, CT

Pleasant Inn Lodge
Rehoboth Beach, DE

Norment-Parry Inn
Orlando, FL

De Loffre House
Columbus, GA

Stovall House
Sautee, GA

Jesse Mount House
Savannah, GA

Stillman's Country Inn
Galena, IL

Redstone Inn
Dubuque, IA

Almeda's B&B Inn
Tonganoxie, KS

Lafitte Guest House
New Orleans, LA

Lamothe House Hotel
New Orleans, LA

English Meadows Inn
Kennebunkport, ME

Broad Bay Inn & Gallery
Waldoboro, ME

Strawberry Inn
New Market, MD

Glenburn
Taneytown, MD

Beechwood Inn
Cape Cod—Barnstable, MA

Cyrus Kent House
Cape Cod—Chatham, MA

Wingate Crossing
Cape Cod—North Falmouth, MA

Inn on Sea Street
Hyannis, MA

Addison Choate Inn
Rockport, MA

Isaiah Jones Homestead
Sandwich, MA

Raymond House Inn
Port Sanilac, MI

Hamilton Place
Holly Springs, MS

Rosswood Plantation
Lorman, MS

Linden
Natchez, MS

Oak Square Inn
Port Gibson, MS

Borgman's B&B
Arrow Rock, MO

Garth Woodside Mansion
Hannibal, MO

Harding House B&B
Saint Joseph, MO

Inn St. Gemme Beauvais
Sainte Genevieve, MO

Nevada City Hotel
Nevada City, MT

Steele Homestead Inn
Antrim, NH

Inn at Crystal Lake
Eaton Center, NH

Bungay Jar B&B
Franconia, NH

New London Inn
New London, NH

Conover's Bay Head Inn
Bay Head, NJ

Abbey
Cape May, NJ

Mainstay Inn
Cape May, NJ

Queen Victoria
Cape May, NJ

Ashling Cottage
Spring Lake, NJ

Brae Loch Inn
Cazenovia, NY

Rose Inn
Ithaca, NY

Belle Crest House
Shelter Island, NY

**Hist. James R. Webster
Mansion Inn**
Waterloo, NY

Cedar Crest Victorian Inn
Asheville, NC

Cider Mill B&B
Zoar, OH

Cobbler Shop Inn
Zoar, OH

Barley Sheaf Farm B&B Inn
Holicong, PA

Witmer's Tavern
Lancaster, PA

Pineapple Hill
New Hope, PA

Millstone Inn
Schellsburg, PA

Hotel Manisses
Block Island, RI

Vendue Inn
Charleston, SC

Clardy's Guest House
Murfreesboro, TN

Annie's B&B Country Inn
Big Sandy, TX

Pine Colony Inn
Center, TX

Imperial Hotel
Park City, UT

Seven Wives Inn
Saint George, UT

Inn at Woodchuck Hill Farm
Grafton, VT

Governor's Inn
Ludlow, VT

Historic Brookside Farms
Orwell, VT

Lareau Farm Inn
Waitsfield, VT

Village Inn of Woodstock
Woodstock, VT

Mayhurst Inn
Orange, VA

Conyers House
Sperryville, VA

Williamsburg Legacy B&B
Williamsburg, VA

Inn at Narrow Passage
Woodstock, VA

Chelsea Station B&B Inn
Seattle, WA

General Lewis Inn
Lewisburg, WV

Yesterdays Ltd. B&B
Wheeling, WV

Old Rittenhouse Inn
Bayfield, WI

Thorp House Inn
Fish Creek, WI

Boyer Ranch
Savery, WY

Auberge Manoir de Tilly
Saint Antoine de Tilly, PQ

Comfort

Old-fashioned comfort and friendly staff are important to every lodging. These inns have these qualities in abundance.

Aztec B&B
Flagstaff, AZ

Pelican Cove Inn
Carlsbad, CA

Glass Beach B&B Inn
Fort Bragg, CA

Big River Lodge
Mendocino, CA

Dunbar House, 1880
Murphys, CA

Burgundy/Bordeaux House
Napa Valley, CA

Grandmere's Inn
Nevada City, CA

Little Inn on the Bay
Newport Beach, CA

Valley View Citrus Ranch
Orosi, CA

Centrella B&B Inn
Pacific Grove, CA

Cinnamon Bear
Saint Helena, CA

Balboa Park Inn
San Diego, CA

Edgemont Inn
San Diego, CA

B&B Inn
San Francisco, CA

Monte Cristo
San Francisco, CA

B&B San Juan
San Juan Bautista, CA

Old Yacht Club Inn
Santa Barbara, CA

Olive House
Santa Barbara, CA

Cottenwood House
Estes Park, CO

Brewery Inn
Silver Plume, CO

Alma House
Silverton, CO

Inn at Chester
Chester, CT

Under Mountain Inn
Salisbury, CT

Small Wonder B&B
Wilmington, DE

Kenwood Inn
Saint Augustine, FL

Foley House Inn
Savannah, GA

'417' Haslam-Fort House
Savannah, GA

Harrison House B&B
Naperville, IL

Davis House
Crawfordsville, IN

Checkerberry Inn
Goshen, IN

Patchwork Quilt Inn
Middlebury, IN

Hotel—The Frenchmen
New Orleans, LA

Lamothe House Hotel
New Orleans, LA

Castlemaine Inn
Bar Harbor, ME

Windward House
Camden, ME

Cape Neddick House
Cape Neddick, ME

Castine Inn
Castine, ME

1802 House
Kennebunkport, ME

Dock Square Inn
Kennebunkport, ME

Old Fort Inn
Kennebunkport, ME

Gosnold Arms
New Harbor, ME

Newcastle Inn
Newcastle, ME

COMFORT, *Cont'd*

Broad Bay Inn & Gallery
Waldoboro, ME

Squire Tarbox Inn
Wiscasset, ME

Jo-Mar B&B on the Ocean
York Beach, ME

Kemp House Inn
Saint Michaels, MD

Newel Post
Uniontown, MD

Grafton Inn
Cape Cod—Falmouth, MA

Honeysuckle Hill
Cape Cod—West Barnstable, MA

Point Way Inn
Edgartown, MA

Pistachio Cove
Lakeville, MA

Haus Andreas
Lee, MA

Amity House
Lenox, MA

Walker House
Lenox, MA

Whistler's Inn
Lenox, MA

Corner House
Nantucket, MA

Seven Sea Street
Nantucket, MA

Rocky Shores Inn & Cottages
Rockport, MA

Coach House Inn
Salem, MA

Golden Goose
Tyringham, MA

Bayberry Inn
Vineyard Haven, MA

Raymond House Inn
Port Sanilac, MI

Thorwood
Hastings, MN

Canturbury Inn B&B
Rochester, MN

Steele Homestead Inn
Antrim, NH

Haverhill Inn
Haverhill, NH

Forest, A Country Inn
Intervale, NH

Benjamin Prescott Inn
Jaffrey, NH

Crab Apple Inn
Plymouth, NH

Snowvillage Inn
Snowville, NH

Conover's Bay Head Inn
Bay Head, NJ

Holly House
Cape May, NJ

Queen Victoria
Cape May, NJ

Normandy Inn
Spring Lake, NJ

Lamplight Inn
Lake Luzerne, NY

Lanza's Country Inn
Livingston Manor, NY

Genesee Country Inn
Mumford, NY

Fourth Ward B&B
Charlotte, NC

Mountain High
Glenville, NC

Baird House
Mars Hill, NC

Colonel Ludlow House
Winston-Salem, NC

Chanticleer Inn
Ashland, OR

Country Willows Inn
Ashland, OR

Edinburgh Lodge B&B
Ashland, OR

Romeo Inn
Ashland, OR

Country Lane B&B
Lakeside, OR

Corbett House B&B
Portland, OR

Spring House
Airville, PA

Covered Bridge Inn
Ephrata, PA

Smithton Inn
Ephrata, PA

Wedgwood B&B Inn
New Hope, PA

Edgeworth Inn
Monteagle, TN

Blue Mtn Mist Country Inn
Sevierville, TN

Old Miners' Lodge
Park City, UT

Pullman B&B Inn
Provo, UT

Zion House
Springdale, UT

Inn at Sunderland
Arlington, VT

Inn at Long Last
Chester, VT

Garrison Inn
East Burke, VT

1811 House
Manchester, VT

Brookside Meadows
Middlebury, VT

Stone House Inn
North Thetford, VT

Golden Kitz Lodge
Stowe, VT

Raspberry Patch
Stowe, VT

Lareau Farm Inn
Waitsfield, VT

Nutmeg Inn
Wilmington, VT

Juniper Hill Inn
Windsor, VT

King Carter Inn
Irvington, VA

Fassifern B&B
Lexington, VA

Conyers House
Sperryville, VA

North Garden Inn
Bellingham, WA

Palmer's Chart House
Deer Harbor, WA

Saratoga Inn
Langley, WA

Inn at Swifts Bay
Lopez Island, WA

Chelsea Station
Seattle, WA

Galer Place B&B
Seattle, WA

Shelburne Inn
Seaview, WA

Swallow's Nest
Vashon Island, WA

Abendruh B&B Swiss-style
Belleville, WI

Viroqua Heritage Inn
Viroqua, WI

Tres Palmas Guest House
San Juan, PR

Conference

Small conferences can be very productive when held in the inns listed below, all of which have the facilities you need and the quiet and opportunity, too, for the fellowship you require.

Power's Mansion Inn
Auburn, CA

Fairview Manor
Ben Lomond, CA

Bear Wallow Resort
Boonville, CA

Valley Lodge
Carmel Valley, CA

Cobblestone
Carmel, CA

Murphy's Inn
Grass Valley, CA

Old Milano Hotel
Gualala, CA

San Benito House
Half Moon Bay, CA

Sorensen's Resort
Hope Valley, CA

Julian Gold Rush Hotel
Julian, CA

Eagles Landing
Lake Arrowhead, CA

Hill House Inn
Mendocino, CA

Gosby House
Pacific Grove, CA

Old St. Angela Inn
Pacific Grove, CA

Briggs House Inn
Sacramento, CA

Archbishop's Mansion
San Francisco, CA

Edward II Inn
San Francisco, CA

Jackson Court
San Francisco, CA

Petite Auberge
San Francisco, CA

Madison Street Inn
Santa Clara, CA

Babbling Brook Inn
Santa Cruz, CA

Darling House
Santa Cruz, CA

Trojan Horse Inn
Sonoma, CA

Vineyard Inn
Sonoma, CA

St. George Hotel
Volcano, CA

Hotel Lenado
Aspen, CO

Wanek's Lodge
Estes Park, CO

New Sheridan Hotel
Telluride, CO

Inn at Chapel West
New Haven, CT

Susina Plantation Inn
Thomasville, GA

Manoa Valley Inn
Honolulu, Oahu, HI

Beaumont Inn
Harrodsburg, KY

Rokeby Hall
Lexington, KY

High Meadows B&B
Eliot, ME

Goose Cove Lodge
Sunset, ME

East Wind Inn & Mtg.Hse.
Tenants Harbor, ME

Inn at Buckeystown
Buckeystown, MD

Strawberry Inn
New Market, MD

Corner House
Nantucket, MA

Wood Farm
Townsend, MA

Dunleith
Natchez, MS

Schwegmann House B&B Inn
Washington, MO

Watson Manor Inn
North Platte, NE

Lyme Inn
Lyme, NH

New London Inn
New London, NH

Whistling Swan Inn
Stanhope, NJ

Troutbeck
Amenia, NY

Brae Loch Inn
Cazenovia, NY

Balsam House
Chestertown, NY

Inn at Cooperstown
Cooperstown, NY

Geneva on the Lake
Geneva, NY

Genesee Country Inn
Mumford, NY

Garnet Hill Lodge
North River, NY

Lords Proprietors' Inn
Edenton, NC

Swag
Waynesville, NC

Inn at Honey Run
Millersburg, OH

Shelter Harbor Inn
Westerly, RI

The Graustein Inn
Knoxville, TN

Bullis House Inn
San Antonio, TX

Old Miners' Lodge
Park City, UT

CONFERENCE, *Cont'd*

Village Inn of Bradford
Bradford, VT

Kedron Valley Inn
South Woodstock, VT

Ten Acres Lodge
Stowe, VT

Lareau Farm Inn
Waitsfield, VT

Wallingford Inn
Wallingford, VT

Hermitage Inn
Wilmington, VT

Admiral's Hideaway
Anacortes, WA

La Conner Country Inn
La Conner, WA

Countryside
Summit Point, WV

Decor

Distinctive decor and unusual architecture are always a pleasure. Enjoy them in these inns.

Marks House Inn
Prescott, AZ

Graham's B&B Inn
Sedona, AZ

Williams House Inn
Hot Springs, AR

Union Hotel
Benicia, CA

Mount View Hotel
Calistoga, CA

Carter House
Eureka, CA

Gingerbread Mansion
Ferndale, CA

Saint Orres
Gualala, CA

Blackthorne Inn
Inverness, CA

Old World Inn
Napa, CA

Grandmere's Inn
Nevada City CA

Green Gables Inn
Pacific Grove, CA

James Blair House
Placerville, CA

Morey Mansion B&B Inn
Redlands, CA

Driver Mansion Inn
Sacramento, CA

Villa St. Helena
Saint Helena, CA

Alamo Square Inn
San Francisco, CA

Inn on Castro
San Francisco, CA

Monte Cristo
San Francisco, CA

Sherman House
San Francisco, CA

Willows B&B Inn
San Francisco, CA

Bayberry Inn
Santa Barbara, CA

Sovereign at Santa Monica Bay
Santa Monica, CA

Gables
Santa Rosa, CA

Casa Madrona Hotel
Sausalito, CA

Trojan Horse Inn
Sonoma, CA

Oleander House
Yountville, CA

Hotel Lenado
Aspen, CO

Pikes Peak Paradise
Colorado Springs, CO

The Lovelander
Loveland, CO

Sandford/Pond House
Bridgewater, CT

Chimney Crest Manor
Bristol, CT

Palmer Inn
Mystic, CT

Bailey House
Fernandina Beach, FL

Watson House
Key West, FL

De Loffre House
Columbus, GA

Wedgwood B&B
Hamilton, GA

Ballastone Inn
Savannah, GA

Rock House
Morgantown, IN

Redstone Inn
Dubuque, IA

Die Heimat Country Inn
Homestead, IA

Mintmere Plantation House
New Iberia, LA

Columns Hotel
New Orleans, LA

Hotel—The Frenchmen
New Orleans, LA

Lamothe House Hotel
New Orleans, LA

Brannon-Bunker Inn
Damariscotta, ME

Greenville Inn
Greenville, ME

Captain Lord Mansion
Kennebunkport, ME

Walker Wilson House
Topsham, ME

White Swan Tavern
Chestertown, MD

Ashley Manor
Barnstable, MA

Bradford Inn & Motel
Chatham, MA

Farmhouse at Nauset Beach
East Orleans, MA

The Gables Inn
Lenox, MA

Farmhouse
Orleans, MA

Amelia Payson Guest House
Salem, MA

Stephen Daniels House
Salem, MA

Kemah Guest House
Saugatuck, MI

Maplewood Hotel
Saugatuck, MI

Grand View Lodge
Brainerd, MN

Chatsworth B&B
Saint Paul, MN

Burn
Natchez, MS

Dunleith
Natchez, MS

Anchuca
Vicksburg, MS

Coach Light B&B
Saint Louis, MO

Walnut Street B&B
Springfield, MO

Nevada City Hotel
Nevada City, MT

Bel-Horst Inn
Belgrade, NE

Manor on Golden Pond
Holderness, NH

Wildflowers Guest House
North Conway, NH

Mt. Adams Inn
North Woodstock, NH

Abbey
Cape May, NJ

Bedford Inn
Cape May, NJ

Benn Conger Inn
Groton, NY

Lake Keuka Manor
Hammondsport, NY

Genesee Country Inn
Mumford, NY

H.W. Allen Villa B&B
Troy, OH

Grandview B&B
Astoria, OR

Huntington Manor
Corvallis, OR

Corbett House B&B
Portland, OR

Farm Fortune
New Cumberland, PA

Two Meeting Street Inn
Charleston, SC

Villa de La Fontaine B&B
Charleston, SC

Annie's B&B Country Inn
Big Sandy, TX

Historical Hudspeth House
Canyon, TX

Pullman B&B Inn
Provo, UT

Seven Wives Inn
Saint George, UT

Brigham Street Inn
Salt Lake City, UT

South Shire Inn
Bennington, VT

Reluctant Panther
Manchester, VT

Fassifern B&B
Lexington, VA

Mayhurst Inn
Orange, VA

Catlin-Abbott House
Richmond, VA

Old Rittenhouse Inn
Bayfield, WI

Eagle Harbor Inn & Cot.
Ephraim, WI

Franklin Victorian
Sparta, WI

Gray Goose B&B
Sturgeon Bay, WI

Viroqua Heritage Inn
Viroqua, WI

Tucker's B&B
Victoria, BC

Family Fun

Be sure to check this list if you're traveling with your brood of six. The inns below are ideal for a family fun vacation.

Lynx Creek Farm B&B
Prescott, AZ

Ames Lodge
Mendocino, CA

Kelsall's Ute Creek Ranch
Ignacio, CO

E.T.'s B&B
Paonia, CO

Shady Maples
Bar Harbor, ME

Hiram Alden Inn
Belfast, ME

Windward House
Camden, ME

Gosnold Arms
New Harbor, ME

Goose Cove Lodge
Sunset, ME

B&B at Ludington
Ludington, MI

Pentwater Inn
Pentwater, MI

DownOver Holdings
Arrow Rock, MO

Richardson House B&B
Jamesport, MO

Lone Mountain Ranch
Big Sky, MT

Cottonwood Ranch Retreat
Roberts, MT

Franconia Inn
Franconia, NH

Dana Place Inn
Jackson, NH

Nestlenook Inn
Jackson, NH

Lake Shore Farm
Northwood, NH

Cordova
Ocean Grove, NJ

All Breeze Guest Farm
Barryville, NY

FAMILY FUN, *Cont'd*

Corner Birches B&B
Lake George, NY

Carefree Cottages
Nags Head, NC

Hugging Bear Inn
Chester, VT

Tyler Place on L. Champlain
Highgate Springs, VT

Johnny Seesaw's
Peru, VT

Liberty Hill Farm
Rochester, VT

Angie's Guest Cottage
Virginia Beach, VA

Teton Tree House
Jackson Hole, WY

Boyer Ranch
Savery, WY

Tucker's B&B
Victoria, BC

Fishing

Nothing like a good catch. These inns are near the haunts of the really big ones. Fishing over, head back to the inn and tell tall tales to fellow enthusiasts.

Gustavus Inn
Gustavus, AK

River Beauty B&B
Talkeetna, AK

Matlick House
Bishop, CA

Sorensen's Resort
Hope Valley, CA

Charles & Charlaine Carter
Monterey, CA

Jean's Riverside B&B
Oroville, CA

River Rock Inn
Placerville, CA

Faulkner House
Red Bluff, CA

Darling House
Santa Cruz, CA

Parrish's Country Sq.
Berthoud, CO

Harbour Inne
Mystic, CT

1735 House
Amelia Island, FL

Hopp-Inn Guest House
Marathon, FL

McBride's B&B
Irwin, ID

Redfish Lake Lodge
Stanley, ID

Squire Tarbox Inn
Wiscasset, ME

Dockside Guest Qtrs.
York, ME

Jonah Williams Inn
Annapolis, MD

Blue Lake Lodge B&B
Mecosta, MI

Grand View Lodge
Brainerd, MN

Lone Mountain Ranch
Big Sky, MT

Izaak Walton Inn
Essex, MT

Old Pioneer Garden
Imlay, NV

Inn at Crystal Lake
Eaton Center, NH

Inn at Coit Mtn.
Newport, NH

Cranmore Mtn. Lodge
North Conway, NH

Follansbee Inn
North Sutton, NH

Mt. Adams Inn
North Woodstock, NH

The Cable House
Rye, NH

Chestnut Hill
Milford, NJ

Thousand Islands Inn
Clayton, NY

Lakeside Terrace B&B
Dundee, NY

Garnet Hill Lodge
North River, NY

Langdon House B&B
Beaufort, NC

Randolph House Inn
Bryson City, NC

Gingerbread Inn
Chimney Rock, NC

Tar Heel Inn
Oriental, NC

Blue Boar Lodge
Robbinsville, NC

Holmes Sea Cove B&B
Brookings, OR

Tu Tu Tun Lodge
Gold Beach, OR

The Handmaiden's Inn
Grants Pass, OR

La Anna Guest House
Cresco, PA

Hickory Bridge Farm
Orrtanna, PA

Fairfield-By-The-Sea
Green Hill, RI

John C. Rogers House
Center, TX

Meadeau View Lodge
Cedar City, UT

Old Miners' Lodge
Park City, UT

Hill Farm Inn
Arlington, VT

Churchill House Inn
Brandon, VT

Rowell's Inn
Chester, VT

Tyler Place on L. Champlain
Highgate Springs, VT

Inn at Manchester
Manchester, VT

Black Lantern Inn
Montgomery Village, VT

North Hero House
North Hero, VT

Lake St. Catherine Inn
Poultney, VT

Lareau Farm Inn
Waitsfield, VT

Highland Inn
Monterey, VA

Turtleback Farm Inn
Eastsound, WA

Tudor Inn
Port Angeles, WA

Orchard Hill Inn
White Salmon, WA

Greenbrier River Inn
Caldwell, WV

Cobblestone-on-The-Ohio
Sistersville, WV

The Griffin Inn
Ellison Bay, WI

Viroqua Heritage Inn
Viroqua, WI

Gingerbread House
Mayne Island, BC

Sunnymeade House Inn
Victoria, BC

Northern Wilderness Lodge
Plaster Rock, NB

Gardens

Ah, to while away an hour in a lovely garden. What could be more relaxing? These inns are renowned for their lush gardens.

Culbert House Inn
Amador City, CA

Gramma's B&B Inn
Berkeley, CA

Wayside Inn
Calistoga, CA

Holiday House
Carmel, CA

Monte Verde Inn
Carmel, CA

Sandpiper Inn
Carmel, CA

Vintage Towers Inn
Cloverdale, CA

Gingerbread Mansion
Ferndale, CA

Old Milano Hotel
Gualala, CA

Mill Rose
Half Moon Bay, CA

Gate House Inn
Jackson, CA

B&B Inn at La Jolla
La Jolla, CA

Casa Laguna Inn
Laguna Beach, CA

Victorian Farmhouse
Little River, CA

Brewery Gulch Inn
Mendocino, CA

Hill House Inn
Mendocino, CA

Goose & Turrets
Montara, CA

House of 1000 Flowers
Monte Rio, CA

Jabberwock
Monterey, CA

Country Garden Inn
Napa, CA

Villa Royale Inn
Palm Springs, CA

Harvest Inn
Saint Helena, CA

Union Street Inn
San Francisco, CA

Babbling Brook Inn
Santa Cruz, CA

Cliff Crest Inn
Santa Cruz, CA

Seal Beach Inn
Seal Beach, CA

Victorian Garden Inn
Sonoma, CA

Barretta Gardens Inn
Sonora, CA

Sutter Creek Inn
Sutter Creek, CA

Country House Inn
Templeton, CA

Byron Randall's GH
Tomales, CA

Howard Creek Ranch
Westport, CA

Butternut Farm
Glastonbury, CT

Eaton Lodge
Key West, FL

Merlinn Guesthouse
Key West, FL

Wicker Guesthouse
Key West, FL

St. Francis Inn
Saint Augustine, FL

Jesse Mount House
Savannah, GA

Liberty Inn
Savannah, GA

Manor House Inn
Bar Harbor, ME

Hartwell House
Ogunquit, ME

Shiverick Inn
Edgartown, MA

Seekonk Pines Inn
Great Barrington, MA

Apple Tree Inn
Lenox, MA

Corner House
Nantucket, MA

The Summer House
Nantucket—Siasconset, MA

Stephen Daniels House
Salem, MA

Summer House
Siasconset, MA

GARDENS, *Cont'd*

Hutchinson's Garden B&B
Northport, MI

Dunleith
Natchez, MS

Hope Farm
Natchez, MS

Old Red Inn
North Conway, NH

Martin Hill Inn
Portsmouth, NH

Woolverton Inn
Stockton, NJ

Back of the Beyond
Colden, NY

Geneva on the Lake
Geneva, NY

Swiss Hutte
Hillsdale, NY

Rose Mansion & Gardens
Rochester, NY

Bakers B&B
Stone Ridge, NY

Sage Cottage
Trumansburg, NY

Ray House B&B
Asheville, NC

Edinburgh Lodge B&B
Ashland, OR

Endicott Gardens
Gold Beach, OR

Salisbury House
Allentown, PA

Garrott's B&B
Cowansville, PA

Bishop's Rocking Horse Inn
Gettysburg, PA

Back Street Inn
New Hope, PA

Villa de La Fontaine B&B
Charleston, SC

Annie's B&B Country Inn
Big Sandy, TX

Inn on the Common
Craftsbury Common, VT

Brookside Meadows
Middlebury, VT

Trail's End
Wilmington, VT

Juniper Hill Inn
Windsor, VT

Conyers House
Sperryville, VA

Schnauzer Crossing B&B
Bellingham, WA

General Lewis Inn
Lewisburg, WV

Boydville, Inn at Martinsburg
Martinsburg, WV

Rose Garden Guest House
Vancouver, BC

Golf

Tee off, walk and relax, then head back to your cozy inn. What could be nicer?

Dry Creek Inn
Auburn, CA

Charles & Charlaine Carter
Monterey, CA

Napa Inn
Napa, CA

Crown Hotel
Inverness, FL

Victoria Place
Koloa, HI

Guesthouse at Volcano
Volcano, HI

Kinter House Inn
Corydon, IN

Teetor House Inn/Hagerstown
Hagerstown, IN

Old Hoosier House
Knightstown, IN

Grane's Fairhaven Inn
Bath, ME

Green Acres Inn
Canton, ME

Chebeague Isl. Inn
Chebeague Island, ME

1802 House
Kennebunkport, ME

Harbourside Inn
Northeast Harbor, ME

Sign of the Unicorn
Rockport, ME

Squire Tarbox Inn
Wiscasset, ME

Hynson Tourist Home
Easton, MD

Snow Hill Inn
Snow Hill, MD

Ashfield Inn
Ashfield, MA

Four Winds
South Yarmouth, MA

Village House
Jackson, NH

Davenport Inn
Jefferson, NH

Jefferson Inn
Jefferson, NH

Birchwood Inn
Temple, NH

The Kenilworth
Spring Lake, NJ

Brae Loch Inn
Cazenovia, NY

Geneva on the Lake
Geneva, NY

Over Yonder B&B
Black Mountain, NC

Buttonwood Inn
Franklin, NC

Greystone Inn
Lake Toxaway, NC

Pine Ridge Inn
Mount Airy, NC

Tar Heel Inn
Oriental, NC

Fairway Inn
Spruce Pine, NC

Hallcrest Inn
Waynesville, NC

Heath Lodge
Waynesville, NC

Palmer House
Waynesville, NC

Paradise Ranch Inn
Grants Pass, OR

Pine Knoll Inn
Aiken, SC

Main House
Texarkana, TX

Peterson's B&B
Monroe, UT

Old Miners' Lodge
Park City, UT

Barrows House
Dorset, VT

Governor's Inn
Ludlow, VT

1811 House
Manchester, VT

Manchester Highlands Inn
Manchester, VT

Golden Stage Inn
Proctorsville, VT

1860 House
Stowe, VT

Valley Inn
Waitsfield, VT

Beaver Pond Farm Inn
Warren, VT

Beaver Pond Farm Inn
Warren, VT

Blush Hill House
Waterbury, VT

Vine Cottage Inn
Hot Springs, VA

Eagle Harbor Inn & Cot.
Ephraim, WI

Sunnymeade House Inn
Victoria, BC

Gourmet

An excellent meal can add a lot to your stay. The inns listed here are particularly celebrated for their fine cuisine.

Williams House Inn
Hot Springs, AR

Union Hotel
Benicia, CA

Mount View Hotel
Calistoga, CA

Carter House
Eureka, CA

Old Milano Hotel
Gualala, CA

Madrona Manor
Healdsburg, CA

Pelican Inn
Muir Beach, CA

Sherman House
San Francisco, CA

Old Yacht Club Inn
Santa Barabra, CA

Casa Madrona Hotel
Sausalito, CA

Inn at Chester
Chester, CT

Homestead Inn
Greenwich, CT

Copper Beech Inn
Ivorytown, CT

David Finney Inn
New Castle, DE

Chalet Suzanne Country Inn
Lake Wales, FL

Smith House
Dahlonega, GA

Stovall House
Sautee, GA

Patchwork Quilt Inn
Middlebury, IN

Inn at Stone City
Anamosa, IA

Talbot Tavern
Bardstown, KY

Columns Hotel
New Orleans, LA

Hotel-The Frenchmen
New Orleans, LA

Penobscot Meadows
Belfast, ME

Camden Harbour Inn
Camden, ME

Crocker House Country Inn
Hancock, ME

Le Domaine Restaurant & Inn
Hancock, ME

Dock Square Inn
Kennebunkport, ME

White Barn Inn
Kennebunkport, ME

Squire Tarbox Inn
Wiscasset, ME

Bramble Inn
Cape Cod—Brewster, MA

Old Manse Inn
Cape Cod—Brewster, MA

Turning Point Inn
Great Barrington, MA

Haus Andreas
Lee, MA

Country Inn
Princeton, MA

Bayberry Inn
Vineyard Haven, MA

Inn at Duck Creeke
Wellfleet, MA

Schumacher's Hotel
New Prague, MN

Canturbury Inn B&B
Rochester, MN

der Klingerbau Inn
Hermann, MO

Bel-Horst Inn
Belgrade, NE

Bradford Inn
Bradford, NH

Staffords in the Field
Chocurua, NH

Inn at Crystal Lake
Eaton Center, NH

New London Inn
New London, NH

Stonehurst Manor
North Conway, NH

Follansbee Inn
North Sutton, NH

Mt. Adams Inn
North Woodstock, NH

Chesterfield Inn
West Chesterfield, NH

GOURMET, *Cont'd*

Bay Head Sands
Bay Head, NJ

El Paradero
Santa Fe, NM

Troutbeck
Amenia, NY

Crabtree's Kittle House
Chappaqua, NY

Balsam House
Chestertown, NY

Hedges House
East Hampton, NY

Benn Conger Inn
Groton, NY

Swiss Hutte
Hillsdale, NY

Rose Inn
Ithaca, NY

Interlaken Lodge
Lake Placid, NY

Taughannock Farms Inn
Trumansburg, NY

Hist. James R. Webster Mansion Inn
Waterloo, NY

Randolph House Inn
Bryson City, NC

Eli Olive's Inn & Rest.
Smithfield, NC

Grandview Lodge
Waynesville, NC

Paradise Ranch Inn
Grants Pass, OR

Steamboat Inn
Steamboat, OR

Spring House
Airville, PA

Overlook Inn
Canadensis, PA

Pine Barn Inn
Danville, PA

Golden Pheasant Inn
Erwinna, PA

Academy Street B&B
Hawley, PA

Black Bass Hotel
Lumberville, PA

Longswamp B&B
Mertztown, PA

Centre Bridge Inn
New Hope, PA

Inn at Phillips Mill
New Hope, PA

White Cloud
Newfoundland, PA

Wycombe Inn
Wycombe, PA

Hotel Manisses
Block Island, RI

Shelter Harbor Inn
Westerly, RI

The Willcox Inn
Aiken, SC

Phelp's House Inn & Rest.
Highlands, TN

Inn on the River
Glen Rose, TX

Old Miners' Lodge
Park City, UT

Arlington Inn
Arlington, VT

Craftsbury Inn
Craftsbury, VT

Blueberry Hill Inn
Goshen, VT

Vermont Inn
Killington, VT

Governor's Inn
Ludlow, VT

Reluctant Panther
Manchester, VT

Red Clover Inn
Mendon, VT

Middletown Springs Inn
Middletown Springs, VT

Old Newfane Inn
Newfane, VT

Norwich Inn
Norwich, VT

Millbrook Inn
Waitsfield, VT

Colonial House
Weston, VT

Inn at Weston
Weston, VT

Channel Bass Inn
Chincoteague, VA

Kenmore Inn
Fredericksburg, VA

Ravenswood Inn
Mathews, VA

Guest House B&B
Greenbank, WA

Shelburne Inn
Seaview, WA

Gite du Mont Albert
Saint Anne des Mont, PQ

Auberge Manoir de Tilly
Saint Antoine de Tilly, PQ

Historic

Inns situated in historic buildings or locales hold a special appeal for many people. The following is a sampling.

Webster House
Alameda, CA

Mine House Inn
Amador City, CA

Power's Mansion Inn
Auburn, CA

Coloma Country Inn
Coloma, CA

City Hotel
Columbia, CA

Rock Haus
Del Mar, CA

Gingerbread Mansion
Ferndale, CA

Heirloom Inn
Ione, CA

Julian Gold Rush Hotel
Julian, CA

Victorian Farmhouse
Little River, CA

Eastlake Inn
Los Angeles, CA

Meadow Creek Ranch
Mariposa, CA

Headlands Inn
Mendocino, CA

Ink House
Saint Helena, CA

Washington Square Inn
San Francisco, CA

B&B San Juan
San Juan Bautista, CA

Thistle Dew Inn
Sonoma, CA

Oak Hill Ranch
Tuolumne, CA

St. George Hotel
Volcano, CA

House of Yesteryear
Ouray, CO

Teller House Hotel
Silverton, CO

New Sheridan Hotel
Telluride, CO

Killingworth Inn
Killingworth, CT

Red Brook Inn
Old Mystic, CT

French Renaissance House
Plainfield, CT

Old Riverton Inn
Riverton, CT

Spring Garden B&B
Laurel, DE

David Finney Inn
New Castle, DE

William Penn Guest House
New Castle, DE

Historic Island Hotel
Cedar Key, FL

Bailey House
Fernandina Beach, FL

Ritz-Ocala's Historic Inn
Ocala, FL

York House
Mountain City, GA

Stovall House
Sautee, GA

B&B Inn
Savannah, GA

Comer House
Savannah, GA

Brick House B&B
Goodfield, IL

Old World Inn
Spillville, IA

Almeda's B&B Inn
Tonganoxie, KS

Talbot Tavern
Bardstown, KY

Tezcuco Plantation Village
Darrow, LA

Mintmere Plantation House
New Iberia, LA

Parkview Guest House
New Orleans, LA

Blue Hill Inn
Blue Hill, ME

The Elms
Camden, ME

Norumbega Inn
Camden, ME

Lincoln House Inn
Dennysville, ME

Weston House
Eastport, ME

High Meadows B&B
Eliot, ME

Bagley House
Freeport, ME

Captain Lord Mansion
Kennebunkport, ME

Homeport Inn
Searsport, ME

Gibson's Lodging
Annapolis, MD

White Swan Tavern
Chestertown, MD

Inn at Perry Cabin
Saint Michaels, MD

Piper House B&B Inn
Sharpsburg, MD

Glenburn
Taneytown, MD

Winchester Country Inn
Westminster, MD

Thomas Huckins House
Barnstable, MA

Thomas Huckins House
Barnstable, MA

Chatham Town House Inn
Cape Cod—Chatham, MA

Cyrus Kent House
Cape Cod—Chatham, MA

Lion's Head Inn
Cape Cod—West Harwich, MA

Easton House
Nantucket, MA

The Penny House
North Eastham, MA

Osterville Fairways Inn
Osterville, MA

Perryville Inn
Rehoboth, MA

Egremont Inn
South Egremont, MA

Merrell Tavern Inn
South Lee, MA

Colonial House Inn
Yarmouth Port, MA

Old Wing Inn
Holland, MI

National House Inn
Marshall, MI

Clifford Lake Hotel
Stanton, MI

Archer House
Northfield, MN

Millsaps Buie House
Jackson, MS

Rosswood Plantation
Lorman, MS

Dunleith
Natchez, MS

Hope Farm
Natchez, MS

Linden
Natchez, MS

Oak Square Inn
Port Gibson, MS

Anchuca
Vicksburg, MS

The Corners
Vicksburg, MS

Borgman's B&B
Arrow Rock, MO

Inn St. Gemme Beauvais
Sainte Genevieve, MO

Six Chimneys
East Hebron, NH

Historic Tavern Inn
Gilmanton, NH

HISTORIC, *Cont'd*

1785 Inn
North Conway, NH

Mt. Adams Inn
North Woodstock, NH

Acorn Lodge
Ossipee, NH

The Cable House
Rye, NH

Captain Mey's Inn
Cape May, NJ

Chestnut Hill
Milford, NJ

Ashling Cottage
Spring Lake, NJ

Casita Chamisa B&B
Albuquerque, NM

Preston House
Santa Fe, NM

Genesee Country Inn
Mumford, NY

Ray House B&B
Asheville, NC

Inn at Brevard
Brevard, NC

King's Arms Inn
New Bern, NC

Oakwood Inn
Raleigh, NC

Cider Mill B&B
Zoar, OH

Haven @ 4th & Park
Zoar, OH

Edinburgh Lodge B&B
Ashland, OR

McCully House Inn
Jacksonville, OR

Inn at Fordhook Farm
Doylestown, PA

Covered Bridge Inn
Ephrata, PA

Osceola Mill House
Gordonville-Intercourse, PA

Ash Mill Farm
Holicong, PA

Witmer's Tavern
Lancaster, PA

Pineapple Inn
Lewisburg, PA

Cameron Estate Inn
Mount Joy, PA

Wedgwood B&B Inn
New Hope, PA

Limestone Inn B&B
Strasburg, PA

Strasburg Village Inn
Strasburg, PA

Bellevue House
Newport, RI

Melville House
Newport, RI

Old Dennis House
Newport, RI

Kings Courtyard Inn
Charleston, SC

Maison DuPre
Charleston, SC

Palmer Home
Charleston, SC

Sword Gate Inn
Charleston, SC

Nicholls-Crook Plantation House
Switzer, SC

Hale Springs Inn
Rogersville, TN

Historic Rugby
Rugby, TN

Gast Haus Lodge
Comfort, TX

Country Cottage Inn
Fredericksburg, TX

J Bar K Ranch B&B
Fredericksburg, TX

Old Miners' Lodge
Park City, UT

Pullman B&B Inn
Provo, UT

Seven Wives Inn
Saint George, UT

Brigham Street Inn
Salt Lake City, UT

National Historic B&B
Salt Lake City, UT

Beauchamp Place
Brandon, VT

Shire Inn
Chelsea, VT

Chester House
Chester, VT

Governor's Inn
Ludlow, VT

1811 House
Manchester, VT

Swift House Inn
Middlebury, VT

Century Past
Newbury, VT

Old Newfane Inn
Newfane, VT

Golden Stage Inn
Proctorsville, VT

Lareau Farm Inn
Waitsfield, VT

West Dover Inn
West Dover, VT

Edgewood Plantation
Charles City, VA

North Bend Plan. B&B
Charles City, VA

La Vista Plantation
Fredericksburg, VA

Wayside Inn
Middletown, VA

Inn at Montross
Montross, VA

Pumpkin House Inn
Mount Crawford, VA

Mayhurst Inn
Orange, VA

High Meadows—Vineyard Inn
Scottsville, VA

1763 Inn
Upperville, VA

Shelburne Inn
Seaview, WA

Greenbrier River Inn
Caldwell, WV

Prospect Hill B&B
Gerrardstown, WV

General Lewis Inn
Lewisburg, WV

Boydville, Inn at Martinsburg
Martinsburg, WV

Plough Inn B&B
Madison, WI

Pink Fancy Hotel
Saint Croix, VI

Victoria's Historic Inn
Wolfville, NS

Willow Place Inn
Hudson, PQ

Low Price

The following lodgings are particularly noted for modest pricing. It is possible to obtain a room for $30 or less.

Krafts' Korner
Mobile, AL

Inn at Castle Rock
Bisbee, AZ

Cedar B&B
Flagstaff, AZ

Creekside Inn & Resort
Guerneville, CA

Pelennor B&B
Mariposa, CA

Rockridge B&B
Oakland, CA

Jean's Riverside B&B
Oroville, CA

Casa Arguello
San Francisco, CA

Edward II Inn
San Francisco, CA

Pensione San Francisco
San Francisco, CA

Little Red Ski Haus
Aspen, CO

Snow Queen Lodge
Aspen, CO

Purple Mountain Lodge
Crested Butte, CO

Midwest Country Inn
Limon, CO

House of Yesteryear
Ouray, CO

St. Elmo Hotel
Ouray, CO

Alma House
Silverton, CO

Teller House Hotel
Silverton, CO

Colonial House
Edgewater, FL

Idaho City Hotel
Idaho City, ID

The Publick House
Metamora, IN

Die Heimat Country Inn
Homestead, IA

Old World Inn
Spillville, IA

Almeda's B&B Inn
Tonganoxie, KS

B&B and the Country
Wakefield, KS

Doe Run Inn
Brandenburg, KY

Marquette House
New Orleans, LA

Shady Maples
Bar Harbor, ME

Old Tavern Inn
Litchfield, ME

Captain's House B&B
Newcastle, ME

Farmhouse Inn
Rangeley, ME

Crab Apple Acres Inn
The Forks, ME

Kawanhee Inn
Weld, ME

Wood Farm
Townsend, MA

Governor's Inn
Lexington, MI

Blue Lake Lodge B&B
Mecosta, MI

Evelo's B&B
Minneapolis, MN

Mission Mountain B&B
Saint Ignatius, MT

Bel-Horst Inn
Belgrade, NE

Old Pioneer Garden
Imlay, NV

Ellis River House
Jackson, NH

Lake Shore Farm
Northwood, NH

Casa del Rey
Los Alamos, NM

Orange Street B&B
Los Alamos, NM

Plum Tree
Taos, NM

All Breeze Guest Farm
Barryville, NY

Edge of Thyme
Candor, NY

Sunrise Inn B&B
Hancock, NY

Corner Birches B&B
Lake George, NY

Napoli Stagecoach Inn
Little Valley, NY

Tibbitt's House
Rensselaer, NY

Spencertown Guests
Spencertown, NY

Country Road Lodge
Warrensburg, NY

Womble Inn
Brevard, NC

Mountain High
Glenville, NC

Brookside Lodge
Lake Junaluska, NC

Sunset Inn
Lake Junaluska, NC

Portage House
Akron, OH

Coach House Inn
Ashland, OR

Out of the Blue B&B
Independence, OR

Winding Glen Farm
Christiana, PA

La Anna Guest House
Cresco, PA

Villamayer
Jamestown, PA

Groff Tourist Farm
Kinzer, PA

Runnymede Farm
Quarryville, PA

Homestead Lodging
Smoketown, PA

Lakeside Farm
Webster, SD

Clardy's Guest House
Murfreesboro, TN

Nolan House Inn
Waverly, TN

Bullis House Inn
San Antonio, TX

Cardinal Cliff
San Antonio, TX

Main House
Texarkana, TX

LOW PRICE, Cont'd

Rio Grande B&B
Weslaco, TX

Seven Wives Inn
Saint George, UT

Poplar Manor
Bethel, VT

Garrison Inn
East Burke, VT

Inn at Manchester
Manchester, VT

Valley House Inn
Orleans, VT

Fox Stand Inn
Royalton, VT

Fiddler's Green Inn
Stowe, VT

Weathervane Lodge
West Dover, VT

Schroder Haus
Wilmington, VT

Palmer's Chart House
Deer Harbor, WA

Crawford's Country Corner
Lost Creek, WV

Arcade Guest House
San Juan, PR

Mesa Creek Ranch
Millarville, AB

Sea Breeze Lodge
Hornby Island, BC

Silver Creek Guest House
Salmon Arm, BC

Deerbank Farm
Morris, MB

Reid's Farm
Centreville, NB

Cailwick Babbling Brook
Riverside, NB

Village Inn
Trinity, NF

Shining Tides
Granville Ferry, NS

Blue Heron Inn
Pugwash, NS

Glenroy Farm
Braeside, ON

Australis Guest House
Ottawa, ON

Beatrice Lyon Guest House
Ottawa, ON

Obanlea Farm
Cornwall, PEI

Sherwood Acres
Kensington, PEI

Auberge Laketree
Knowlton, PQ

Chateau Beauvalion
Mont Tremblant, PQ

Armor Inn
Montreal, PQ

Edale Place
Portneuf, PQ

Luxury

These establishments are famed for their luxurious appointments, special attention to creature comforts and style.

Dairy Hollow House
Eureka Springs, AR

Gramma's B&B Inn
Berkeley, CA

Carriage House
Laguna Beach, CA

Mountain Home Inn
Mill Valley, CA

Forest Manor
Napa Valley, CA

Doryman's Inn
Newport Beach, CA

Villa St. Helena
Saint Helena, CA

Jackson Court
San Francisco, CA

Sherman House
San Francisco, CA

West Lane Inn
Ridgefield, CT

Ballastone Inn
Savannah, GA

Charlton Court
Savannah, GA

Foley House Inn
Savannah, GA

Rokeby Hall
Lexington, KY

Lamothe House Hotel
New Orleans, LA

Soniat House
New Orleans, LA

Harraseeket Inn
Freeport, ME

Captain Lord Mansion
Kennebunkport, ME

Deerfield Inn
Deerfield, MA

Country Inn
Princeton, MA

Burn
Natchez, MS

Linden
Natchez, MS

Oak Square Inn
Port Gibson, MS

Stonehurst Manor
North Conway, NH

Mainstay Inn
Cape May, NJ

Preston House
Santa Fe, NM

Brae Loch Inn
Cazenovia, NY

Geneva on the Lake
Geneva, NY

**Hist. James R. Webster
Mansion Inn**
Waterloo, NY

Romeo Inn
Ashland, OR

Overlook Inn
Canadensis, PA

Guesthouse at Doneckers
Ephrata, PA

Admiral Fitzroy Inn
Newport, RI

The Willcox Inn
Aiken, SC

Elliott House Inn
Charleston, SC

Kings Courtyard Inn
Charleston, SC

Vendue Inn
Charleston, SC

Brigham Street Inn
Salt Lake City, UT

Emerald City Inn
Seattle, WA

Captain's Palace
Victoria, BC

Northumberland Heights Country Inn
Cobourg, ON

Jakobstettel Guest House
Saint Jacobs, ON

Le Chateau De Pierre
Quebec City, PQ

Manoir Ste. Genevieve
Quebec City, PQ

Nature

Nature lovers, alert! Be your fancy ornithology or whale watching, these inns will speak to your heart.

Homer B&B/Seekins
Homer, AK

River Beauty B&B
Talkeetna, AK

Arizona Mountain Inn
Flagstaff, AZ

Graham's B&B Inn
Sedona, AZ

Bolinas Villa
Bolinas, CA

Cazanoma Lodge
Cazadero, CA

Elk Cove Inn
Elk, CA

Narrow Gauge Inn
Fish Camp, CA

Grey Whale Inn
Fort Bragg, CA

Creekside Inn & Resort
Guerneville, CA

Sorensen's Resort
Hope Valley, CA

Meadow Creek Ranch
Mariposa, CA

Ames Lodge
Mendocino, CA

House of 1000 Flowers
Monte Rio, CA

Forest Manor
Napa Valley, CA

Bear Valley Inn
Olema, CA

Inn at Shallow Creek Farm
Orland, CA

River Rock Inn
Placerville, CA

Horseshore Farm Cottage
Point Reyes, CA

Marsh Cottage
Point Reyes, CA

Twain Harte's B&B
Twain Harte, CA

Wilbur Hot Springs
Williams, CA

Outlook Lodge
Green Mountain Falls, CO

Pelican Inn
Carrabelle, FL

Laurel Ridge
Dahlonega, GA

York House
Mountain City, GA

Little St. Simons Island
Saint Simons Island, GA

Holmes Retreat B&B
Pocatello, ID

Stillwaters Country Inn
Galena, IL

Manor House Inn
Bar Harbor, ME

Anchor Watch B&B
Boothbay Harbor, ME

Lincoln House Inn
Dennysville, ME

Inn at Harbor Head
Kennebunkport, ME

Cedarholm Cottages
Lincolnville, ME

Breezemere Farm Inn
South Brooksville, ME

Goose Cove Lodge
Sunset, ME

Kawanhee Inn
Weld, ME

Bayview Inn B&B
Wells, ME

Jonah Williams Inn
Annapolis, MD

Wades Point Inn On Bay
McDaniel, MD

Inn at Duck Creeke
Wellfleet, MA

Pincushion Mountain B&B
Grand Marais, MN

Pincushion Mtn. B&B
Grand Marais, MN

Kettle Falls Hotel
Orr, MN

Lone Mountain Ranch
Big Sky, MT

Izaak Walton Inn
Essex, MT

Dana Place Inn
Jackson, NH

Province Inn
Strafford, NH

Bear Mtn. Guest Ranch
Silver City, NM

Plum Tree
Taos, NM

Benn Conger Inn
Groton, NY

NATURE, Cont'd

R.M. Farm
Livingston Manor, NY

Genesee Falls Hotel
Portageville, NY

Taughannock Farms Inn
Trumansburg, NY

Over Yonder B&B
Black Mountain, NC

Randolph House Inn
Bryson City, NC

Trestle House Inn
Edenton, NC

Havenshire Inn
Hendersonville, NC

Berkley Center Country Inn
Ocracoke, NC

Snowbird Mtn. Lodge
Robbinsville, NC

Heath Lodge
Waynesville, NC

Swag
Waynesville, NC

Inn at Honey Run
Millersburg, OH

Mirror Pond House
Bend, OR

Holmes Sea Cove B&B
Brookings, OR

Capt. Quarters B&B
Coos Bay, OR

Backroads B&B
Eugene, OR

Fair Winds B&B
Gold Beach, OR

Barkheimer House
Hood River, OR

Mountain Shadows B&B
Zig Zag, OR

Swiss Woods B&B
Lititz, PA

Millstone Inn
Schellsburg, PA

Woodhill Farms Inn
Washington Crossing, PA

Alford House
Chattanooga, TN

Windhover
Gatlinburg, TN

Historic Rugby
Rugby, TN

Bluff B&B
Bluff, UT

Meadeau View Lodge
Cedar City, UT

Zion House
Springdale, UT

Long Run Inn
Bristol, VT

Three Mountain Inn
Jamaica, VT

Village Inn
Jay, VT

Inn at Long Trail
Killington, VT

Troutbrook Lodge
Killington, VT

Johnny Seesaw's
Peru, VT

Green Mtn. Tea Room
South Wallingford, VT

Lareau Farm Inn
Waitsfield, VT

Vine Cottage Inn
Hot Springs, VA

Trillium House
Nellysford, VA

Burrow's Bay B&B
Anacortes, WA

Growly Bear B&B
Ashford, WA

Mountain Meadows Inn
Ashford, WA

Eagles Nest Inn B&B
Langley, WA

West Shore Farm B&B
Lummi Island, WA

Puget View Guesthouse
Olympia, WA

Whispering Pines
Spokane, WA

Orchard Hill Inn
White Salmon, WA

Spahn's Big Horn Mtn. Lodge
Big Horn, WY

Teton Tree House
Jackson Hole, WY

Estate Zootenvaal
Saint John, VI

Selene's
Saint John, VI

Black Cat Guest Ranch
Hinton, AB

Yellow Point Lodge
Ladysmith, BC

Sooke Harbour House
Sooke, BC

Village Inn
Trinity, NF

Shining Tides
Granville Ferry, NS

Outstanding

The following inns are some which, due to attention to detail, amenities and ambience, are truly outstanding.

Graham's B&B Inn
Sedona, AZ

Dairy Hollow House
Eureka Springs, AR

Williams House Inn
Hot Springs, AR

Union Hotel
Benicia, CA

Grey Whale Inn
Fort Bragg, CA

Pelican Inn
Muir Beach, CA

Dunbar House, 1880
Murphys, CA

Forest Manor
Napa Valley, CA

Beazley House
Napa, CA

Briggs House Inn
Sacramento, CA

Britt House
San Diego, CA

Mansion Hotel
San Francisco, CA

Seal Beach Inn
Seal Beach, CA

Bishopsgate Inn
East Haddam, CT

St. Francis Inn
Saint Augustine, FL

Inn at Stone City
Anamosa, IA

Beaumont Inn
Harrodsburg, KY

Grenoble House Inn
New Orleans, LA

Hotel Maison de Ville
New Orleans, LA

Soniat House
New Orleans, LA

Cambridge House B&B
Cambridge, MA

Bramble Inn
Cape Cod—Brewster, MA

Whalewalk Inn
Cape Cod—Eastham, MA

Stephen Daniels House
Salem, MA

Schumacher's Hotel
New Prague, MN

Bel-Horst Inn
Belgrade, NE

Franconia Inn
Franconia, NH

Snowvillage Inn
Snowville, NH

Abbey
Cape May, NJ

Barnard-Good House
Cape May, NJ

Mainstay Inn
Cape May, NJ

Lodge at Cloudcroft
Cloudcroft, NM

Grant Corner Inn
Santa Fe, NM

Troutbeck
Amenia, NY

1770 House
East Hampton, NY

Adelphi Hotel
Saratoga Springs, NY

**Hist. James R. Webster
Mansion Inn**
Waterloo, NY

Woodfield Inn
Flat Rock, NC

Havenshire Inn
Hendersonville, NC

Swag
Waynesville, NC

Coachaus
Allentown, PA

Overlook Inn
Canadensis, PA

Admiral Benbow Inn
Newport, RI

Battery Carriage House
Charleston, SC

Indigo Inn
Charleston, SC

Planters Inn
Charleston, SC

Green Trails Inn
Brookfield, VT

Inn on the Common
Craftsbury Common, VT

Black River Inn
Ludlow, VT

Governor's Inn
Ludlow, VT

Galer Place B&B
Seattle, WA

Kalorama Guest House
Washington, DC

Romance

Ah, romance! These inns offer hideaway, a peaceful space in which to be together and let the world go by.

Crescent Moon Townhouse
Eureka Springs, AR

Dairy Hollow House
Eureka Springs, AR

Knickerbocker Mansion
Big Bear Lake, CA

Happy Landing Inn
Carmel, CA

Elk Cove Inn
Elk, CA

Gingerbread Mansion
Ferndale, CA

Heirloom Inn
Ione, CA

Murphy's Jenner-by-the-Sea
Jenner, CA

Big River Lodge
Mendocino, CA

Cypress House
Mendocino, CA

Pelican Inn
Muir Beach, CA

**Maison Bleu Country
French B&B**
Pacific Grove, CA

Cricket Cottage
Point Reyes Station, CA

East Brother Light Station
Point Richmond, CA

Creekwood
Saint Helena, CA

Villa St. Helena
Saint Helena, CA

ROMANCE, *Cont'd*

Grand Cottages
San Pedro, CA

Glenborough Inn
Santa Barbara, CA

Simpson House Inn
Santa Barbara, CA

Babbling Brook Inn
Santa Cruz, CA

Cliff Crest Inn
Santa Cruz, CA

Seal Beach Inn
Seal Beach, CA

Jameson's
Sonora, CA

Holden House—1902
Colorado Springs, CO

Queen Anne Inn
Denver, CO

Simsbury 1820 House
Simsbury, CT

York House
Mountain City, GA

Liberty Inn
Savannah, GA

Inn at Stone City
Anamosa, IA

Cornstalk Hotel
New Orleans, LA

Lafitte Guest House
New Orleans, LA

Ledgelawn Inn
Bar Harbor, ME

Blue Hill Inn
Blue Hill, ME

Chebeague Isl. Inn
Chebeague Island, ME

Ashley Manor
Barnstable, MA

Beechwood Inn
Cape Cod—Barnstable, MA

Old Sea Pines Inn
Cape Cod—Brewster, MA

Chatham Town House Inn
Cape Cod—Chatham, MA

Country Inn
Princeton, MA

Stephen Daniels House
Salem, MA

Wedgewood Inn
Yarmouth Port, MA

Victorian Villa
Union City, MI

Schumacher's Hotel
New Prague, MN

Rosswood Plantation
Lorman, MS

Oak Square Inn
Port Gibson, MS

Augustine River Bluff Farm
New Haven, MO

Gunstock Inn
Gilford, NH

Greenfield Inn
Greenfield, NH

Barnard-Good House
Cape May, NJ

Gingerbread House
Cape May, NJ

Chestnut Hill
Milford, NJ

Sierra Mesa Lodge
Alto, NM

La Posada de Taos
Taos, NM

Inn at Shaker Mill
Canaan, NY

Geneva on the Lake
Geneva, NY

Rose Inn
Ithaca, NY

Lamplight Inn
Lake Luzerne, NY

Mt. Tremper Inn
Mount Tremper, NY

Oliver Loud's Inn
Pittsford, NY

Village Victorian Inn
Rhinebeck, NY

**Hist. James R. Webster
Mansion Inn**
Waterloo, NY

Rowan Oak House
Salisbury, NC

Livingston Mansion Inn
Jacksonville, OR

Sandlake Country Inn
Sandlake, OR

Spring House
Airville, PA

Canadensis Old Village Inn
Canadensis, PA

Clarion River Lodge
Cook Forest, PA

Brinley Victorian Inn
Newport, RI

Willows of Newport
Newport, RI

Two Meeting Street Inn
Charleston, SC

Windhover
Gatlinburg, TN

Durham House
Houston, TX

Black River Inn
Ludlow, VT

Governor's Inn
Ludlow, VT

Inn at Manchester
Manchester, VT

Manchester Highlands Inn
Manchester, VT

Reluctant Panther
Manchester, VT

White House
Wilmington, VT

Edgewood Plantation
Charles City, VA

Silver Thatch Inn
Charlottesville, VA

Channel Bass Inn
Chincoteague, VA

Ravenswood Inn
Mathews, VA

Conyers House
Sperryville, VA

Guest House B&B
Greenbank, WA

White Lace Inn
Sturgeon Bay, WI

Captain's Palace
Victoria, BC

Faye & Eric's B&B
Summerside, PEI

Skiing

These inns share a proximity to downhill or cross-country skiing. Nothing like coming back from an exhilarating day on the slopes to a warm, cozy fire.

Gold Mtn. Manor Country Inn
Big Bear City, CA

Sorensen's Resort
Hope Valley, CA

Snow Goose B&B Inn
Mammoth Lakes, CA

Jameson's
Sonora, CA

River Ranch
Tahoe City, CA

Capt.'s Alpenhaus Inn
Tahoma, CA

Little Red Ski Haus
Aspen, CO

Ullr Lodge
Aspen, CO

Hardy House B&B Inn
Georgetown, CO

Kelsall's Ute Creek Ranch
Ignacio, CO

Eagle River Inn
Minturn, CO

New Sheridan Hotel
Telluride, CO

Busterback Ranch
Ketchum, ID

Noble House
Bridgton, ME

Center Lovell Inn
Center Lovell, ME

Ashfield Inn
Ashfield, MA

Seekonk Pines Inn
Great Barrington, MA

Turning Point Inn
Great Barrington, MA

Birchwood Inn
Lenox, MA

Cornell House
Lenox, MA

Country Cottage B&B
Maple City, MI

Lone Mountain Ranch
Big Sky, MT

Izaak Walton Inn
Essex, MT

Steele Homestead Inn
Antrim, NH

Country Inn at Bartlett
Bartlett, NH

Notchland Inn
Bartlett, NH

Bradford Inn
Bradford, NH

Darby Field Inn
Conway, NH

Chase House
Cornish, NH

Inn at Danbury
Danbury, NH

Franconia Inn
Franconia, NH

Trumbull House
Hanover, NH

Haverhill Inn
Haverhill, NH

Meeting House Inn
Henniker, NH

Dana Place Inn
Jackson, NH

Nestlenook Inn
Jackson, NH

Maple Hill Farm
New London, NH

Cranmore Mtn. Lodge
North Conway, NH

Old Red Inn
North Conway, NH

Sunny Side Inn
North Conway, NH

Follansbee Inn
North Sutton, NH

Mt. Adams Inn
North Woodstock, NH

Meadow Farm B&B
Northwood, NH

Snowvillage Inn
Snowville, NH

Haus Edelweiss B&B
Sunapee, NH

Back of the Beyond
Colden, NY

Geneva on the Lake
Geneva, NY

Benn Conger Inn
Groton, NY

Mt. Tremper Inn
Mount Tremper, NY

Garnet Hill Lodge
North River, NY

Inn on Bacon Hill
Saratoga Springs, NY

La Anna Guest House
Cresco, PA

Meadeau View Lodge
Cedar City, UT

505 Woodside B&B
Park City, UT

Imperial Hotel
Park City, UT

Old Miners' Lodge
Park City, UT

Washington School Inn
Park City, UT

Brigham Street Inn
Salt Lake City, UT

Mountain Hollow B&B Inn
Sandy, UT

Mtn. Hollow B&B
Sandy, UT

Hill Farm Inn
Arlington, VT

Alpenrose Inn
Bondville, VT

Arches Country Inn
Brandon, VT

Long Run Inn
Bristol, VT

Mill Brook B&B
Brownsville, VT

Shire Inn
Chelsea, VT

Greenleaf Inn
Chester, VT

Craftsbury Inn
Craftsbury, VT

Maple Crest Farm
Cuttingsville, VT

Little Lodge
Dorset, VT

Garrison Inn
East Burke, VT

SKIING, *Cont'd*

Blueberry Hill Inn
Goshen, VT

Village Inn
Jay, VT

Inn at Long Trail
Killington, VT

Vermont Inn
Killington, VT

Blue Gentian Lodge
Londonderry, VT

Country Hare
Londonderry, VT

Black River Inn
Ludlow, VT

Governor's Inn
Ludlow, VT

Okemo Inn
Ludlow, VT

Manchester Highlands Inn
Manchester, VT

Brookside Meadows
Middlebury, VT

Black Lantern Inn
Montgomery Village, VT

Johnny Seesaw's
Peru, VT

Salt Ash Inn
Plymouth Union, VT

Liberty Hill Farm
Rochester, VT

Green Mtn. Tea Room
South Wallingford, VT

1860 House
Stowe, VT

Raspberry Patch
Stowe, VT

The Siebeness
Stowe, VT

Lareau Farm Inn
Waitsfield, VT

Sugartree Country Inn
Warren, VT

Shield Inn
West Dover, VT

Snow Den Inn
West Dover, VT

Weathervane Lodge
West Dover, VT

West Dover Inn
West Dover, VT

Windham Hill Inn
West Townsend, VT

Colonial House
Weston, VT

Riverside Guest House
Woodstock, VT

Vine Cottage Inn
Hot Springs, VA

Tudor Inn
Port Angeles, WA

Jefferson-Day House
Hudson, WI

Schweizer Lodge
Sutton, PQ

Amherst Shore Country Inn
Amherst, NS

Little Inn
Bayfield, ON

Jakobstettel Guest House
Saint Jacobs, ON

Auberge Otter Lake Haus
Huberdeau, PQ

Spas

Hot mineral waters are nature's own relaxant. These inns have a close proximity to, or are, spas.

Williams House Inn
Hot Springs, AR

Brannan Cottage Inn
Calistoga, CA

Culver's Country Inn
Calistoga, CA

Foothill House
Calistoga, CA

Pine Street Inn
Calistoga, CA

Scarlett's Country Inn
Calistoga, CA

White Sulphur Springs Ranch
Clio, CA

Mill Rose
Half Moon Bay, CA

Ojai Manor Hotel
Ojai, CA

Aunt Abigail's Inn
Sacramento, CA

Howard Creek Ranch
Westport, CA

Wilbur Hot Springs
Williams, CA

House of Yesteryear
Ouray, CO

St. Elmo Hotel
Ouray, CO

Poor Farm Country Inn
Salida, CO

Idaho City Hotel
Idaho City, ID

Peterson's B&B
Monroe, UT

Vine Cottage Inn
Hot Springs, VA

Inn at Gristmill
Warm Springs, VA

Folkestone B&B
Berkeley Springs, WV

Maria's Garden & Inn
Berkeley Springs, WV

Manan Island Inn & Spa
Grand Manan, NB

Special

These inns all have an extra special, out of the ordinary something which distinguishes them. We hope you'll agree.

Dairy Hollow House
Eureka Springs, AR
Antique bathtub "big enough for two."

Gingerbread Mansion
Ferndale, CA
Twin clawfoot tubs—"his & her" bubble baths.

Swan-Levine House
Grass Valley, CA
Guests may observe and participate in the fine art of printmaking.

Saint Orres
Gualala, CA
Incredibly beautiful handwrought fantasy building.

Eastlake Inn
Los Angeles, CA
Celebrate a Dickens Christmas in LA's only Victorian B&B.

B.G. Ranch & Inn
Mendocino, CA
Grow own eggs, vegetables & herbs; fluent French & Italian, trout pond, lavish breakfast.

Chichester House B&B
Placerville, CA
Gourmet breakfast served above a gold mine.

East Brother Light Station
Point Richmond, CA
On an island in the middle of San Francisco Bay!

Mansion Hotel
San Francisco, CA
Magic shows and a resident "spirit."

Darling House
Santa Cruz, CA
Oceanside horse drawn carriage rides.

Country House Inn
Templeton, CA
Near Hearst Castle.

Byron Randall's GH
Tomales, CA
Gallery showing Byron Randall's art work; also world's foremost collection of hand-powered potato mashers.

Home Ranch
Clark, CO
Sleigh rides and a herd of llamas.

Jules' Undersea Lodge
Key Largo, FL
World's only undersea lodge.

Susina Plantation Inn
Thomasville, GA
Pretend you're Scarlett O'Hara.

Patchwork Quilt Inn
Middlebury, IN
Meet Amish families on Backroads Tour. Quilt collection.

Inn at Stone City
Anamosa, IA
Moonlight surrey serenade.

Myrtles Plantation
Saint Francisville, LA
On "Mystery Weekends," guests wear period costumes and try to solve historic murders at "America's most haunted house."

Holbrook House
Bar Harbor, ME
Large doll collection.

Greenville Inn
Greenville, ME
Largest seaplane base on the East Coast.

The Keeper's House
Isle Au Haut, ME
Island lighthouse inn with working lighthouse.

Crab Apple Acres Inn
The Forks, ME
Guided whitewater rafting trips on the Kennebec or Dead Rivers, Apr.-Oct.

Spring Bank
Frederick, MD
Wide view from observatory; china collection in use.

Old Manse Inn
Cape Cod—Brewster, MA
During the Civil War, a link to the underground railroad.

Seekonk Pines Inn
Great Barrington, MA
Fresh vegetables for sale in the garden.

Wildwood Inn
Ware, MA
Refreshing "Norman Rockwell" brook-fed swimming hole.

Birk's Goethe St. Gasthaus
Hermann, MO
Mansion Mystery Weekends with local actors and special guests.

Lazy K Bar Ranch
Big Timber, MT
Exclusive use of a horse for your holiday on working dude ranch.

Scottish Lion Inn
North Conway, NH
Highland hospitality amid tartans, Scottish paintings and cuisine.

Mt. Adams Inn
North Woodstock, NH
Unique rock formations called "mummies" in back of inn along the Moosalauki River.

Casita Chamisa B&B
Albuquerque, NM
Archaeologist innkeeper delighted to show guests Pueblo Indian village ruins.

Taos Inn
Taos, NM
Original town well located in the center of the lobby.

Brae Loch Inn
Cazenovia, NY
A wee bit o' Scotland.

Gasho Inn
Central Valley, NY
In 30-acre Japanese theme area with gardens, fish pond, tea houses, etc.

Golden Eagle
Garrison, NY
Film location for the movie "Hello Dolly."

Barkheimer House
Hood River, OR
"Windsurfing capital of the world."

Harry Packer Mansion
Jim Thorpe, PA
"Mystery weekends," adventure packages, Victorian balls.

Pineapple Inn
Lewisburg, PA
Room decorated with furniture from summer palace (London) of Archbishop of Canterbury, c. 1880.

SPECIAL, Cont'd

Wedgwood B&B Inn
New Hope, PA
Attend the Inn School and learn the "inns and outs of innkeeping."

Hugging Bear Inn
Chester, VT
Teddy Bear motif and shop.

Inwood Manor
East Barnet, VT
Canoeing on the Connecticut River from the inn.

Fox Stand Inn
Royalton, VT
Special herd of polled Hereford cattle.

Butternut Inn at Stowe
Stowe, VT
Texas Bar-B-Q Anniversary Party held three weekends in July.

Hermitage Inn
Wilmington, VT
Spring maple sugaring—3500 trees.

Cedar Point Country Inn
North, VA
Raises Arabian horses.

Jordan Hollow Farm Inn
Stanley, VA
Restored colonial horse farm in the Shenandoah Valley—horseback riding, of course!

Nantucket Inn
Anacortes, WA
Handmade quilts.

Maria's Garden & Inn
Berkeley Springs, WV
Miraculous painting of the Virgin Mary.

Spahn's Big Horn Mtn. Lodge
Big Horn, WY
Solar power.

Beulah Land
Treherne, MB
Homegrown, homecooked meals.

Village Inn
Trinity, NF
Cetacean contact experiences with Christine & Peter Beamish.

Shining Tides
Granville Ferry, NS
Near the Bay of Fundy. View the rise and fall of the Annapolis River tides.

Waterlot Inn
New Hamburg, ON
Just the place for a romantic gourmet.

Sports

Sports are an integral part of many people's vacation plans. These inns are noted for their sporting facilities or locales. Be sure to call ahead to see if they have the special facilities you require.

Murphy's Inn
Grass Valley, CA

North Coast Country Inn
Gualala, CA

Twain Harte's B&B
Twain Harte, CA

Victorian Inn
Durango, CO

Wanek's Lodge
Estes Park, CO

Harbour Inne
Mystic, CT

Inn on Lake Waramaug
New Preston, CT

Under Mountain Inn
Salisbury, CT

1735 House
Amelia Island, FL

Center Lovell Inn
Center Lovell, ME

Bittersweet Inn
Walpole, ME

Davis House
Solomons Island, MD

Ship's Inn
Chatham, MA

Grandmother's House
Colrain, MA

Apple Tree Inn
Lenox, MA

Raymond House Inn
Port Sanilac, MI

Gunflint Lodge
Grand Marais, MN

Winters Creek Ranch
Carson City, NV

Highlands Inn
Bethlehem, NH

Sugar Hill Inn
Franconia, NH

Dana Place Inn
Jackson, NH

Ammonoosuc Inn
Lisbon, NH

Cranmore Mtn. Lodge
North Conway, NH

Lake Shore Farm
Northwood, NH

Snowvillage Inn
Snowville, NH

Gregory House
Averill Park, NY

Balsam House
Chestertown, NY

Geneva on the Lake
Geneva, NY

Country Road Lodge
Warrensburg, NY

Randolph House Inn
Bryson City, NC

Greenwood B&B
Greensboro, NC

Ye Olde Cherokee Inn
Kill Devil Hills, NC

Snowbird Mtn. Lodge
Robbinsville, NC

Mast Farm Inn
Valle Crucis, NC

Gateway Lodge
Cooksburg, PA

La Anna Guest House
Cresco, PA

Cherry Mills Lodge
Dushore, PA

Harry Packer Mansion
Jim Thorpe, PA

Inn at Starlight Lake
Starlight, PA

Wycombe Inn
Wycombe, PA

Historic Rugby
Rugby, TN

Meadeau View Lodge
Cedar City, UT

Peterson's B&B
Monroe, UT

Old Miners' Lodge
Park City, UT

Parmenter House
Belmont, VT

Black Bear Inn
Bolton Valley, VT

Churchill House Inn
Brandon, VT

Craftsbury Inn
Craftsbury, VT

Barrows House
Dorset, VT

Kincraft Inn
Hancock, VT

Troutbrook Lodge
Killington, VT

Vermont Inn
Killington, VT

Governor's Inn
Ludlow, VT

Okemo Inn
Ludlow, VT

1811 House
Manchester, VT

Manchester Highlands Inn
Manchester, VT

Red Clover Inn
Mendon, VT

Johnny Seesaw's
Peru, VT

Golden Stage Inn
Proctorsville, VT

Quechee Inn
Quechee, VT

Fox Stand Inn
Royalton, VT

Londonderry Inn
South Londonderry, VT

Gables Inn
Stowe, VT

Snow Den Inn
West Dover, VT

Vine Cottage Inn
Hot Springs, VA

Palmer's Chart House
Deer Harbor, WA

Teton Tree House
Jackson Hole, WY

Quilchena Hotel
Quilchena, BC

Shadow Lawn Inn
Rothesay, NB

Jakobstettel Guest House
Saint Jacobs, ON

Some Favorite B&B Recipes

From the bustling kitchens of Bed & Breakfasts across the country comes this list of distinctive recipes. Some are simple and quick, others are VERY gourmet. All are delicious. Hope you enjoy them as much as we did.

Drinks

Grant Corner Inn, Santa Fe, New Mexico

ORANGE FRAPPE

4 cups fresh squeezed orange juice
1 lemon, squeezed
1 large banana
6 strawberries, fresh or frozen
¼ cup whipping cream
6 ice cubes

Mix ingredients in electric blender on high speed for approximately 1 minute. Serve in frozen stemmed goblets with fresh sprig of mint garnish. Serves 6.

The Okemo Inn, Ludlow, Vermont

HOT SPICED TEA

Combine the following and boil for 5 minutes:

2 cups sugar
2 cups water
2 inch stick of cinnamon
1 tsp. ground allspice
12 whole cloves or
1 ½ tsp. ground cloves

ADD:

4 tsps. loose tea or use 12 tea bags
Let stand for 10 minutes and
strain.

ADD:

1 ½ cups orange juice (4 oranges)
¾ cup lemon juice (2 lemons)
4 quarts hot water

Serve hot in mugs or cups. The spices and tea can be brewed and stored in glass jar in the refrigerator ahead of time... when ready to use, mix with the juices and water, and heat. Serves 50.

Deerfield Inn, Deerfield, Massachussetts

CHRISTMAS WASSAIL

1 cup water	½ tsp. allspice
4 cups sugar	1 stick cinnamon or
1 Tbsp. nutmeg	2 Tbsps. powdered cinnamon
2 tsps. ginger	4 quarts/liters dry sherry
½ tsp. mace	2 cups brandy
6 whole cloves	1 dozen eggs

Combine water, sugar and spices in a saucepan. Bring to full boil for 5 minutes. Heat sherry and brandy almost to boiling, in separate pans. Separate eggs. Beat whites until stiff. Beat yolks until light in color and well mixed. Fold whites into yolks in a large bowl. Mixing quickly, strain sugar/spice mixture into folded eggs. Use a whisk if available. Very gradually, add hot sherry to egg mixture, stirring constantly. Add brandy, stirring. Serves 25-30.

Appetizers

The Lyme Inn, Lyme, New Hampshire

STUFFED MUSHROOMS

Large Mushrooms	¼ tsp. pepper
¼ cup melted butter	½ tsp. chopped onions
1 tsp. salt	1 cup minced clams

Remove stems and prepare mushrooms for stuffing. Chop the stems and add minced clams. Add butter, salt, pepper and onions. Stuff into mushroom caps. Sprinkle with bread crumbs and paprika. Bake at 400⁰ F. for 20 minutes. Serves 12.

The Bramble Inn, Brewster, Cape Cod, Massachussetts

ANGELS ON HORSEBACK

Wrap raw oysters with strips of bacon. Secure each oyster with a toothpick. Broil until bacon is crisply browned, turning once. Allow 3 oysters for each serving as an hors d'oeuvre.

The Parsonage, Santa Barbara, California
HOT CLAM DIP

2 pkg. 8 oz. cream cheese
4 heaping Tbsps. sour cream
4 Tbsps. mayonnaise
1 tsp. onion powder

2—8 oz. cans minced clams, drained
parmesan cheese
dehydrated chives

Spray pie plate or quiche pan. Mix cream cheese, sour cream and mayonnaise. Blend well. Add clams. Pour in pan—sprinkle heavily with parmesan cheese / lightly with chives. Bake in 325° F. oven for 30 minutes. Serve with wheat thins.

Northfield Country House, Northfield, Massachussetts
SQUASH FLOWER FRITTERS

5 Yellow Squash Flowers
   (Summer Squash)
1 ⅓ cups flour
1 tsp. salt

2 eggs
½ cup milk
1 tsp. salad oil

Rinse flowers, pat dry (well) and break into pieces. Combine with all other ingredients. Drop level tablespoonfuls into 3-4 in. heated oil in deep fat fryer or kettle. Fry 5 mins. Serve hot with maple syrup. Serves 5.

Cereal

Breezemere Farm, So. Brooksville, Maine
BREEZEMERE GRANOLA

5 cups uncooked oatmeal
1 cup safflower oil
1 cup honey
1 cup raisins
1 cup other dried fruit pieces
   (Such as currants or apple)

1 cup each:
   sliced almonds
   broken walnuts
   sesame seeds
   unsalted sunflower seeds
   wheat germ
   shredded coconut

Combine oatmeal, nuts, seeds, wheat germ and coconut well. Meld together oil and honey, pour over dry ingredients and mix well. Bake at 325° F. for one hour or until nicely brown. When cool, add raisins and other dried fruit. Serves 12.

Folkestone, Bryson City, North Carolina

GRANDMA'S OATMEAL

2 ½ cups water
1/8 tsp. salt
2 cups oatmeal
2 heaping Tbsps. sugar

½ tsp. cinnamon
5 oz. can condensed milk
3 Tbsp. butter
5 tbsps. brown sugar

Bring water to a boil. Add salt. Stirring constantly, add dry oatmeal gradually. Continue stirring. Add sugar, cinnamon. Cook 1 minute, add condensed milk and reheat to boiling. Pour into serving dish, add butter and brown sugar.

Fruit Dishes

Grane's Fairhaven Inn, Bath, Maine

BANANAS "GRANE"

MIX:

½ cup sour cream
2.Tbsps. Kirsch

1 Tbsp. sugar or honey
2 Tbsps. whipping cream

SERVE atop fresh-cut sliced bananas and serve with fresh strawberry on top. Serves 8

The Okemo Inn, Ludlow, Vermont

FRESH FRUIT COMPOTE

3 medium-large cantaloupes
1 quart fresh blueberries
1 quart fresh red raspberries
1 cup Amaretto liqueur

whipped cream
sliced almonds—toasted
sugar to taste

Cut each cantaloupe in half crosswise. Trim a sliver from the bottom of each half so they sit flat. Scoop out melon rounds (after removing seeds) leaving a clean smooth "cup" for serving. Put halves in nice serving bowls or on nice small plates and set in refrigerator to chill well. Meanwhile, rinse and drain all berries and place them in a large bowl with the cantaloupe balls. Sprinkle enough sugar over fruit to sweeten slightly (strictly optional) and then pour 1 cup Amaretto liqueur over all. Mix all ingredients well but gently—cover and set in refrigerator to chill.

When ready to serve, fill each cantaloupe shell with fruit mixture. Garnish with a healthy serving of whipped cream and then sprinkle the toasted sliced almonds over all. A sprig of fresh mint adds color and zest!

TO TOAST ALMONDS: Spread sliced almonds thinly on a small cookie pan and toast in 350° F. oven until light golden brown—about 8-10 minutes. Serves 6.

Chalet Suzanne, Lake Wales, Florida

BAKED GRAPEFRUIT

½ grapefruit per person
butter (melted)
sugar
cinnamon
chicken livers

flour
salt
pepper

Cut out small center of each grapefruit half and loosen sections. Fill center cavity with melted butter. Sprinkle top with a mixture of cinnamon and sugar (generously). Place under broiler until well browned. To serve, garnish with a chicken liver or two that have been dusted with flour, salt and pepper and sauteed on a hot grill or skillet in butter.

Muffins

Preston House, Santa Fe, New Mexico

ZUCCHINI MUFFINS

3 eggs
2 cups sugar
1 cup vegetable oil
1 Tbsp. vanilla
2 cups loosely packed
   grated zucchini

2 cups flour
1 Tbsp. cinnamon
2 tsps. soda
1 tsp. salt
½ tsp. baking powder
1 cup chopped nuts

Beat eggs until frothy. Beat in sugar, oil and vanilla until mixture is thick or lemon colored. Stir in zucchini. Add flour, cinnamon, soda, salt, and baking powder. Fold in nuts. Pour mix into 2 oiled and floured 8" x 4 ½ " x 3" pans or muffin tins. Fill only half-full as it bubbles and puffs up during baking. Bake at 350º F, 1 hour for large pans or 30 minutes for muffins. Cool in pans 10 minutes. Serves 12.

Deep Creek Inn, Bonners Ferry, Idaho

ENGLISH TEA MUFFINS

2 cups boiling water
5 tsps. soda
2 cups sugar
1 cup shortening
4 eggs
1 quart buttermilk

2 cups chopped dates
1 cup nuts
5 cups flour
4 cups All Bran
1 cup bran flakes
1 tsp. salt

Add eggs to sugar and shortening and beat well. Add buttermilk, dates and nuts, and mix. Add flour, All Bran, bran flakes, and salt. Add soda and water. You can keep in gallon jar for up to 2 weeks in refrigerator—don't stir—dip out as needed. Pour in muffin or cup cake papers—half-full. Bake at 400° F. for 25 minutes. Serves 35-40.

Wildwood Inn, Ware, Massachussetts

WILDWOOD'S TEA SCONES

2 cups sifted flour	⅓ cup butter
2 Tbsp. sugar	1 egg, beaten
3 tsps. baking powder	Approx. ½ - ¾ cup milk
½ tsp. salt	

Preheat oven to 425° F. Sift flour, sugar, baking powder and salt together. Chop in butter with a pastry blender until the flour-coated particles of butter are the size of coarse cornmeal. Add the egg and about ½ cup milk. Stir quickly and lightly until no flour shows. The less milk the better, but add a little if needed to make a soft dough. Grease your hands and turn the dough out onto a floured dish towel. Knead gently 15 times. Cut dough in half. Shape each half into a ball, and press down each one into a round approx. ¼" thick. Cut each into 8 wedges, like a pie — use a floured knife. Place wedges on a greased cookie sheet or pie tin, not allowing sides to touch. Bake for 10-15 min. If you wish them to shine, glaze with lightly beaten egg before baking. Scones should be golden brown when done. Serves 6.

Pancakes

The Inn at Manchester, Vermont

COTTAGE PANCAKES WITH HOT BLUEBERRY SAUCE

1 cup cottage cheese	6 Tbsps. melted butter
4 fresh eggs	1 cup unbleached flour

Mix cottage cheese, eggs and butter with a wisk. Fold in flour. Bake on a medium griddle. Serves 3.
Sauce:

2 cups blueberries	1 tsp. lemon juice
½ cup sugar	1 cup water
1 tsp. cornstarch	

Combine blueberries, sugar, lemon juice and ½ cup water. Cook for four minutes. Add another ½ cup water mixed with cornstarch. Heat to boiling and serve.

Elk Cove Inn, Elk, California

EIERKUCHEN
(German Egg Cakes)

½ cup flour	½ cup buttermilk
¾ tsp. baking powder	6 egg whites
1 Tbsp. sugar	cream of tartar
dash salt	sweet butter
6 egg yolks	flavoring (vanilla, almond)

Put flour, baking powder, sugar, salt, egg yolks, flavoring and buttermilk in a large bowl. Beat. In a separate bowl beat egg whites quite stiff with cream of tartar. Carefully fold into yolk mixture. Preheat griddle to 275-300⁰ F. with a small amount of butter. Spoon onto griddle (spreading dough slightly with side of spoon) making small round pancakes. Flip over when golden brown to bake other side. Top with any kind of fresh berries or applesauce. Fresh huckleberries taste delicious folded into the mixture just before baking. Serves 4.

B & B in Minuteman Country, Lexington, Massachusetts

SWEDISH PANCAKES

2 eggs	¾ cup milk
½ tsp. salt	⅔ cup flour
¼ cup sugar	1 large Tbsp. oil

Beat eggs. Add remaining ingredients (oil last). Mix until smooth. Bake on moderately hot griddle. Serve with butter and syrup. Serves 2.

Egg Dishes

Edison Hill Manor, Stowe, Vermont

L'OMELET HOMARD FORESTIERE
(Omelette with Lobster and Mushrooms)

4 oz. sliced mushrooms	¼ cup heavy cream
1 oz. clarified butter	1 fresh lobster tail, poached,
salt and pepper to taste	shelled and diced
¼ cup good port	freshly grated Parmesan cheese

Saute the mushrooms in butter, season with salt and pepper, stir in port and cream and reduce 50%. Add the lobster and simmer until the meat is hot. In a prepared omelette pan, add some clarified butter, heat pan and add two beaten eggs. Stir briskly with a fork. Add lobster mixture. Fold, sprinkle with Parmesan, garnish plate and serve quickly. Serves 4.

City Hotel, Columbia, California

EGGS WARHOL
(Poached Eggs in Tomato Halves with Avocado Sauce)

8 poached eggs	1 Tbsp. horse radish sauce
4 ripe tomatoes, halved	salt and pepper to taste
3 ripe Haas avocados	1 ½ cups whipped cream
½ to ¾ cup sour cream	chopped pimento for garnish

Shake the seeds and moisture out of the tomato halves, scoop some of the pulp out of each and discard. Place the tomatoes on a baking sheet and sprinkle with salt and pepper, dot each with olive oil. Broil for 4 minutes, or until lightly brown. Set aside and keep warm. Poach the eggs in a large skillet with one tablespoon of salt and one tablespoon of white vinegar in the water. When done, put one egg in each tomato half. Cover with avocado mousseline sauce and garnish with chopped pimento.

Avocado Mouseline Sauce

Add the 3 avocados, sour cream, lemon juice and horse radish in a mixing bowl and whip until smooth. Add salt and pepper to taste. Run the mixture through a food mill or fine wire mesh to remove avocado pulp and lumps. Fold in whipped cream to make the mousseline. Serves 4.

Dairy Hollow House, Eureka Springs, Arkansas

APPLE-BRIE CHEESE OMELETTE

1 Tbsp. melted butter	1 tbsp. light cream or milk
½ crisp, well-flavored apple,	dash salt
peeled, cored, sliced thinly	dash white pepper
2 eggs	2 Tbsps. brie cheese, diced

Saute apple slices gently in butter until soft but not mushy. Prepare an omelette using eggs, cream or milk, salt and white pepper. Cook in omelette pan, pulling up undersides with spatula to allow uncooked egg to run onto the exposed pan and cook. When omelette is no longer runny but not quite done, scatter brie cheese over its surface. Cook a few seconds longer, then scatter cooked apple slices over the cheese. Roll omelette, and serve on warmed plate. Garnish with a fresh strawberry or a slice of raw apple with the peel still on, and a sprig of fresh mint. Serve with homemade bread (we often use wholewheat butterhorns), butter, and homemade jam. Serves 1 (easily doubled or tripled).

Coffee Cakes

Valley View Citrus Ranch, Orosi, California

5 MINUTE COFFEE CAKE

4 Tbsps. butter	1 tsp. cinnamon
½ cup sugar	salt
1 cup flour	½ cup milk
3 tsps. baking powder	1 egg
chopped nuts or coconut	cinnamon sugar

Preheat oven to 375° F. Put butter in pie pan or square baking pan. Sift together sugar, flour, baking powder, cinnamon and salt. Measure milk, drop in egg, stir and add to flour mixture. Add melted butter last, stir, pour into pan. Sprinkle top with chopped nuts (or coconut) and cinnamon sugar. Bake about 25 minutes. Serve warm. Reheats quite well. Serves 6.

Innwood Manor, East Barnet, Vermont

FLORENTINE CORNMEAL CAKE

⅔ cup soft butter	1 egg yolk
2 ⅔ cups powdered sugar	1 ¼ cups cake flour
1 tsp. vanilla	⅓ cup corn meal
2 whole eggs	

Beat butter with sugar until creamy. Beat in vanilla. Add eggs one at a time. Sift and measure cake flour and then mix with corn meal. Add to batter a portion at a time. Blend well after each addition. Grease and dust decorative deerback pan or 4 cup tube pan. Spoon batter into pan—spread evenly. Bake at 325° F. for 1 hr. 15 min. Cool in pan for a few minutes—turn out to wire rack. Sift some powdered sugar over warm cake. Thinly sliced, serves 15.

Pudding Creek Inn, Fort Bragg, California

PUDDING CREEK INN COFFEE CAKE

2 ½ cups flour	½ tsp. salt
1 cup melted butter	6 Tbsps. sugar
2 tsps. baking powder	2 beaten eggs
½ tsp. baking soda	4 Tbsps. flour
1 cup buttermilk	2 Tbsps. butter
2 tsps. vanilla	⅓ cup fruit jam or
1 cup sugar	drained fruit or pie filling

In medium size bowl stir together the flour, sugar, baking powder, baking soda and salt. Make a well in center of dry ingredients. In small bowl combine eggs, melted butter, buttermilk and vanilla. Add to dry ingredients and mix well. Turn batter into greased rectangular pan (approx. 9" x 13"). Drop jam, drained fruit or pie filling by teaspoons atop batter.

In small bowl combine 6 Tbsps. sugar, 4 Tbsps. flour and 2 tsps. butter. Cut until crumbly. Sprinkle crumb mix atop batter. Serves 18.

Quick Bread

Baker's Manor, Ouray, Colorado

POPPY SEED BREAD

2 eggs	1 cup oil
1 cup milk	2 cups flour
1 cup sugar	½ tsp. salt
1 tsp. vanilla	2 tsps. baking powder
poppy seeds	

Beat together eggs, milk, sugar, vanilla and oil until well blended. Then add flour, salt and baking powder. Beat well and add several tablespoons poppy seeds. Pour into 9" x 4" greased and floured pan. Bake at 350º F. for 45-60 minutes.

Country Inn, Harwich Port, Massachussetts

COUNTRY INN LEMON BREAD

⅓ cup butter	½ cup milk
1 cup sugar	¼ tsp. almond extract
2 eggs	1-½ cup flour
rind of 11 lemons, grated	1 tsp. baking powder

Glaze:

Juice of one lemon	⅓ cup sugar

Preheat oven to 350° F. Grease one loaf pan. Cream butter and sugar until light. Add eggs and beat until well combined. Mix milk, grated rind and almond extract together in measuring cup. Mix flour and baking powder together in small bowl. Add dry ingredients and milk mixture. Beat until well mixed. Bake in loaf pan at 350º F. for one hour or until done when tested with a toothpick. Serves 6.

Woodchuck Hill Farm, Grafton, Vermont

BLUEBERRY BOY BAIT
(Blueberry Bread)

2 cups flour	1 cup milk
1 ½ cups sugar	2 eggs
2 tsps. baking powder	2 to 3 cups blueberries
1 tsp. salt	1 cup sugar
⅔ cup margerine or oil	1 tsp. cinnamon

Combine first 7 ingredients and beat 3 minutes. Pour into greased and floured 9" x 13" pan. Arrange on top of batter at least 2 cups of blueberries. Combine sugar with cinnamon and sprinkle on top. Bake 40-50 minutes at 350°F. Can be reheated. Serve with whipped cream as desert or plain for breakfast. Serves 8.

Toppings

The Inn at Weston, Weston, VT.

APPLE BUTTER

5 lbs. apples	1 ½ tsp. ground cloves
2 cups cider	¼ tsp. ground allspice
1 cup sugar	dash of nutmeg
3 tsp. cinnamon	

Wash, stem and core apples; peel and cut into ¼" wedges. Cook apples in cider with sugar. Season with cinnamon, cloves, allspice and nutmeg. Continue cooking till apples are soft but still hold their shape a bit. Cool and refrigerate.
Besides being a delicious addition to toast or muffins, try mixing with sour cream or mayonnaise for a fruit salad dressing.

Trent River Plantation, Pollocksville, North Carolina

PLANTATION FRUIT SPREAD

8 oz. cream cheese, softened	½ pint strawberries, blueberries, bananas, or cranberries (add some sugar)

Beat cream cheese and fruit until creamy. Chill overnight to develop flavor. Spread on fruit bread.

Briar Rose Bed & Breakfast, Boulder, Colorado

LEMON CURD

juice of 6 lemons	12 beaten eggs
grated rind of 6 lemons	2 ½ cups sugar

Combine all ingredients in double boiler. Stir CONSTANTLY over moderate heat until thick. Cool. Store in refrigerator. Good on hot scones, muffins or biscuits.

Sweet Endings

The Lyme Inn, Lyme, New Hampshire

MAPLE MOUSSE

1 Tbsp. gelatin	½ cup light brown sugar
½ cup water	4 egg whites, whipped
4 egg yolks	2 cups heavy cream, whipped
1 cup maple syrup	

Combine gelatin, water, egg yolks and maple syrup over heat (in a double boiler). Use a wire whip to stir out the lumps. Add the brown sugar and continue to whip. Take off heat and allow to cool slightly. Fold in the beaten egg whites and the whipped cream. Pour into champagne glasses and chill. Serves 4.

The Inn at April Point, Campbell River, British Columbia

CARROT CAKE

2 cups sugar	2 cups flour
1 cup Wesson oil	2 tsps. soda
4 eggs	½ tsp. salt
3 cups grated carrots	1 tsp. cinnamon
1 cup shopped nuts	

Beat eggs, add oil and sugar. Mix nuts with flour, soda and other dry ingredients. Add to egg mixture. Add carrots and beat well. Bake in three layers at 350° F. 35-40 minutes.

FROSTING:

1 cube butter	1 8 oz. pkg. cream cheese
1 lb. packed sugar	1 tsp. vanilla

Combine above ingredients until smooth and creamy. Serves 8.

Subscribe To

THE COMPLETE GUIDE'S GAZETTE
Newsletter for B&Bs, Inns,
Guest Houses and Small Hotels

To get all the latest on the North American inn scene, events, tips and news, send $35 for your subscription to this informative newsletter. Inns that subscribe to the Gazette have first priority to a full listing in this guide. Don't forget to include your name and address with your order. Send your order to:

The Complete Guide's Gazette
P.O. Box 20467
Oakland, CA 94620-0467

ON BECOMING AN INNKEEPER

Do you dream of being an innkeeper, meeting and making friends with interesting guests and regaling them with your own special brand of hospitality? Make no mistake, innkeeping is hard work, but it can be very rewarding.

We have prepared a packet of information on resources for prospective innkeepers which we will send you free of charge.

Many people prefer to buy an established inn. If you are interested in buying an inn you may wish to contact the editor of this guide regarding information we have on inns for sale. To receive the resource packet or information on inns for sale, please send your request and a legal size, stamped, self-addressed envelope to:

The Complete Guide to Bed & Breakfasts, Inns & Guesthouses
P.O. Box 20467
Oakland, CA 94620-0467

VOTE

FOR YOUR CHOICE OF INN OF THE YEAR

To the editors of The Complete Guide to Bed & Breakfasts, Inns and Guesthouses in the U.S. and Canada:

I cast my vote for "Inn of the Year" for:

Name of Inn _____

Address _____

_____

Phone _____

Reasons _____

_____

_____

I would also like to (please check one):

____ Recommend a new Inn   ____ Comment

____ Critique   ____ Suggest

Name of Inn _____

Address _____

_____

Phone _____

Comment _____

_____

_____

Please send your entries to:
The Complete Guide to Bed & Breakfast Inns
P.O. Box 20467
Oakland, CA 94620 0467

OTHER BOOKS FROM JOHN MUIR PUBLICATIONS

22 Days Series: Travel Itinerary Planners
These pocket-size guides are a refreshing departure from ordinary guidebooks. Each author has in-depth knowledge of the region covered and offers 22 carefully tested daily itineraries. Included are not only "must see" attractions but also little-known villages and hidden "jewels" as well as valuable general information. 128 to 144 pp., $7.95 each

22 Days in Alaska by Pamela Lanier (28-68-0)
22 Days in the American Southwest by Richard Harris (28-88-5)
22 Days in Asia by Roger Rapoport and Burl Willes (65-17-3)
22 Days in Australia by John Gottberg (65-03-3)
22 Days in California by Roger Rapoport (28-93-1)
22 Days in China by Gaylon Duke and Zenia Victor (28-72-9)
22 Days in Europe by Rick Steves (65-05-X)
22 Days in France by Rick Steves (65-07-6)
22 Days in Germany, Austria & Switzerland by Rick Steves (65-02-5)
22 Days in Great Britain by Rick Steves (28-67-2)
22 Days in Hawaii by Arnold Schuchter (28-92-3)
22 Days in India by Anurag Mathur (28-87-7)
22 Days in Japan by David Old (28-73-7)
22 Days in Mexico by Steve Rogers and Tina Rosa (65-04-1)
22 Days in New England by Anne E. Wright (28-96-6)
22 Days in New Zealand by Arnold Schuchter (28-86-9)
22 Days in Norway, Denmark & Sweden by Rick Steves (28-83-4)
22 Days in the Pacific Northwest by Richard Harris (28-97-4)
22 Days in Spain & Portugal by Rick Steves (65-06-8)
22 Days in the West Indies by Cyndy and Sam Morreale (28-74-5)

"Kidding Around" Travel Guides for Children
Written for kids eight years of age and older. Generously illustrated in two colors with imaginative characters and images. Each guide is an adventure to read and a treasure to keep.
Kidding Around San Francisco, Rosemary Zibart (65-23-8) 64 pp., $9.95
Kidding Around Washington, D.C., Anne Pedersen (65-25-4) 64 pp., $9.95
Kidding Around London, Sarah Lovett (65-24-6) 64 pp., $9.95

All-Suite Hotel Guide: The Definitive Directory, Pamela Lanier
Pamela Lanier, author of The Complete Guide to Bed & Breakfasts, Inns & Guesthouses, now provides the discerning traveler with a listing of over 600 all-suite hotels. (65-08-4) 285 pp., $13.95

Asia Through the Back Door, Rick Steves and John Gottberg
Provides information and advice you won't find elsewhere—including how to overcome culture shock, bargain in marketplaces, observe Buddhist temple etiquette, and even how to eat noodles with chopsticks! (28-58-3) 336 pp., $13.95

Buddhist America: Centers, Practices, Retreats, Don Morreale
The only comprehensive directory of Buddhist centers, this guide includes first-person narratives of individuals' retreat experiences. (28-94-X) 312 pp., $12.95

Bus Touring: Charter Vacations, U.S.A, Stuart Warren with Douglas Bloch
For many people, bus touring is the ideal, relaxed, and comfortable way to see America. Covers every aspect of bus touring to help passengers get the most pleasure for their money. (28-95-8) 200 pp., $9.95

Catholic America: Self-Renewal Centers and Retreats, Patricia Christian-Meyers
Complete directory of over 500 self-renewal centers and retreats in the United States and Canada. (65-20-3) 325 pp., $13.95

Complete Guide to Bed & Breakfasts, Inns & Guesthouses in the United States and Canada, 1989-90 Edition, Pamela Lanier
Newly revised and the most complete directory available, with over 5,000 listings in all 50 states, 10 Canadian provinces, Puerto Rico, and the U.S. Virgin Islands. (65-09-2) 520 pp., $14.95

Elegant Small Hotels: A Connoisseur's Guide, Pamela Lanier
This lodging guide for discriminating travelers describes hotels characterized by exquisite rooms and suites and personal service par excellence. (65-10-6) 230 pp., $14.95

Europe 101: History & Art for the Traveler, Rick Steves and Gene Openshaw
The first and only jaunty history and art book for travelers makes castles, palaces, and museums come alive. (28-78-8) 372 pp., $12.95

Europe Through the Back Door, Rick Steves
For people who want to enjoy Europe more and spend less money doing it. In this revised edition, Steves shares more of his well-respected insights. (28-84-2) 404 pp., $12.95
Doubleday and Literary Guild Book Club Selection.

Gypsying After 40: A Guide to Adventure and Self-Discovery, Bob Harris
Retirees Bob and Megan Harris offer a witty and informative guide to the "gypsying" life-style that has enriched their lives and can enrich yours. Their message is: "Anyone can do it!" (28-71-0) 312 pp., $12.95

The Heart of Jerusalem, Arlynn Nellhaus
Arlynn Nellhaus draws on her vast experience in and knowledge of Jerusalem to give travelers a rare inside view and practical guide to the Golden City. (28-79-6) 312 pp., $12.95

Mona Winks: Self-Guided Tours of Europe's Top Museums, Rick Steves and Gene Openshaw
Here's a guide that will save you time, shoe leather, and tired muscles. It is designed for people who want to get the most out of visiting the great museums of Europe. (28-85-0) 450 pp., $14.95

The On and Off the Road Cookbook, Carl Franz and Lorena Havens
A multitude of delicious alternatives to the usual campsite meals. (28-27-3) 272 pp., $8.50

The People's Guide to Mexico, Carl Franz
This classic guide shows the traveler how to handle just about any situation that might arise while in Mexico.
"The best 360-degree coverage of traveling and short-term living in Mexico that's going."—*Whole Earth Epilog* (28-99-0) 587 pp., $15.95

The People's Guide to RV Camping in Mexico, Carl Franz and Lorena Havens
This revised guide focuses on the special pleasures and challenges of RV travel in Mexico. Includes a complete campground directory. (28-91-5) 304 pp., $13.95

The Shopper's Guide to Mexico, Steve Rogers and Tina Rosa
The only comprehensive handbook for shopping in Mexico, this guide ferrets out little-known towns where the finest handicrafts are made and offers tips on shopping techniques. (28-90-7) 200 pp., $9.95

Traveler's Guide to Asian Culture, Kevin Chambers
An accurate and enjoyable guide to the history and culture of this diverse continent. (65-14-9) 356 pp., $13.95

Traveler's Guide to Healing Centers and Retreats in North America, Martine Rudee and Jonathan Blease
Over 300 listings offer a wide range of healing centers—from traditional to new age. (65-15-7) 224 pp., $11.95

Undiscovered Islands of the Caribbean, Burl Willes
For the past decade, Burl Willes has been tracking down remote Caribbean getaways. Here he offers complete information on 32 islands. (28-80-X) 220 pp., $12.95

Automotive Repair Manuals
Each JMP automotive manual gives clear step-by-step instructions together with illustrations that show exactly how each system in the vehicle comes apart and goes back together. They tell everything a novice or experienced mechanic needs to know to perform periodic maintenance, tune-ups, troubleshooting, and repair of the brake, fuel and emission control, electrical, cooling, clutch, transmission, driveline, steering and suspension systems and even rebuild the engine.
How to Keep Your VW Alive (65-12-2) 410 pp., $17.95
How to Keep Your Golf/Jetta/Rabbit Alive (65-21-1) 420 pp., $17.95
How to Keep Your Honda Car Alive (28-55-9) 272 pp., $17.95
How to Keep Your Subaru Alive (65-11-4) 420 pp., $17.95
How to Keep Your Toyota Pick-Up Alive (28-89-3) 400 pp., $17.95
How to Keep Your Datsun/Nissan Alive (28-65-6) 544 pp., $17.95
How to Keep Your Honda ATC Alive (28-45-1) 236 pp., $14.95

Other Automotive Books

The Greaseless Guide to Car Care Confidence: Take the Terror out of Talking to Your Mechanic, Mary Jackson
Teaches the reader about all of the basic systems of an automobile. (65-19-X) 200 pp., $14.95

Off-Road Emergency Repair & Survival, James Ristow
Glove compartment guide to troubleshooting, temporary repair, and survival. (65-26-2) 150 pp., $9.95

Road & Track's Used Car Classics, edited by Peter Bohr
Features over 70 makes and models of enthusiast cars built between 1953 and 1979. (28-69-9) 272 pp., $12.95

Ordering Information

Fill in the order blank. Be sure to add up all of the subtotals at the bottom of the order form and give us the address whither your order is to be whisked.

Postage & Handling

Your books will be sent to you via UPS (for U.S. destinations), and you will receive them in approximately 10 days from the time that we receive your order. Include $2.75 for the first item ordered and $.50 for each additional item to cover shipping and handling costs. UPS shipments to post office boxes take longer to arrive; if possible, please give us a street address.

For airmail within the U.S., enclose $4.00 per book for shipping and handling.

All foreign orders will be shipped surface rate. Please enclose $3.00 for the first item and $1.00 for each additional item. Please inquire for airmail rates.

Method of Payment

Your order may be paid by check, money order, or credit card. We cannot be responsible for cash sent through the mail.

All payments must be made in U.S. dollars drawn on a U.S. bank. Canadian postal money orders in U.S. dollars are also acceptable.

For VISA, MasterCard, or American Express orders, use the order form or call (505)982-4078. Books ordered on American Express cards can be shipped only to the billing address of the cardholder. Sorry, no C.O.D.'s. Residents of sunny New Mexico, add 5.625% tax to the total.

Back Orders

We will back order all forthcoming and out-of-stock titles unless otherwise requested.

All prices subject to change without notice.

Address all orders and inquiries to: John Muir Publications
P.O. Box 613
Santa Fe, NM 87504   (505)982-4078

ITEM NO.			TITLE	EACH	QUAN.	TOTAL
		•				
		•				
		•				
		•				
		•				

Postage & handling (see ordering information)* _____

New Mexicans please add 5.625% tax _____

Total Amount Due _____

Credit Card Number: _____

Expiration Date: _____ Daytime telephone _____

Name _____

Address _____

City _____ State _____ Zip _____

Signature X _____

Required for Credit Card Purchases